GLORY & GOVERNMENT

CHICAGO'S CITY HALL

100

Edward M. Burke and Thomas J. O'Gorman

HORTO PRESS

HORTO
PRESS

Edited by Thomas J. O'Gorman, Maxwell Mueller,
Michael Synowiecki, and Erin Waitz
Produced by Horto Press
Designed by Sam Silvio, Silvio Design, Inc.
Printed by Rider Dickerson Press, Maywood Illinois

ISBN: 978-0-615-33322-9

Front Cover
Chicago City Hall (1916)
Holabird & Root

Back Cover
Chicago City Hall's Green Roof
© Chicago Photo Lab

Endsheets
Inside front
Original blueprint of Chicago's City Hall
exterior massing by Holabird & Roche
Courtesy, Chicago Department of General Services

Tall ships and wooden streets–
Chicago's other shore–The River Front © 1860

Inside back
Thomas J. O'Gorman
Detail of Chicago's City Hall at 100, 2009
Acrylic on linen, 60 x 40 inches

1920's Vintage postcard of Chicago's City Hall

Contents

For our parents
Joe and Ann Burke
Moss and Eileen O'Gorman

When most I wink, then
do my eyes best see.
W. Shakespeare

The mother art is architecture.
Without an architecture of our own we
have no soul of our own civilization.
Frank Lloyd Wright

Acknowledgements

We are grateful for all of those whose hands joined us in this enterprise. Their skill and effort helped to shape this project and polish our efforts.

Sean Sweaney for his computers skills and knowledge of the classical world.

Conor Lucas, Maxwell Mueller, Michael Synowiecki and **Paul Weaver** for their research abilities and noses for clues in libraries and hidden places.

President **Gary Johnson** of the Chicago History Museum for his many kindnesses and historical interest in our project. And **Rob Medina** of the CHM photo duplication department who did so much to advance the quality of this work.

Sam Silvio whose remarkable artistry actually shaped the artistic elegance of this book's design.

Andrea Miller, Matthew Link and **Erin Waitz** of the Committee on Finance for their millions of kindness and noses for research where no thing remains hidden.

Commissioner **Mary Dempsey** of the Chicago Public Library and the remarkable staff of the **Municipal Reference Library,** there, and the many pieces of Chicago history they found for us.

Kathy Taylor of Rider Dickerson Press who assisted so much in the physical fabrication of this book.

Pat Pyszka at the Chicago City Hall Photo Services Department.

Tim Samuelson, cultural historian at the Department of Cultural Affairs of the City of Chicago for his keen eye and editorial assistance.

Jim Miller, principal, Holabird & Root for access to remarkable photographs.

Kate Sansome, Office of the Mayor.

Anthony Pascente, City of Chicago, Department of General Services.

Prologue
By Thomas J. O'Gorman

*"Architecture, of all the arts, is the one which acts
the most slowly, but the most surely, on the soul."*
Ernest Dimnet

Chicago's City Hall looms larger-than-life from an
urban footprint that is one full city block square.
The clean massing of the exterior granite replete with
forty-two six-story Corinthian columns immediately
seizes the viewer, creating an overwhelming sense
of size and space.

*Who does not know that the first law of historical
writing is the truth?*—Marcus Tullius Cicero said two
millennia ago. That was wise advice in Ancient Rome
and it is even more important for us today. This has
been the ethic under which all our work on this
Centennial History of Chicago's City Hall was filtered.

With a deliberate municipal majesty, the architecture of this century-old structure has determined not only the perceptions of what takes place within, but also what shapes the character of the exterior streetscape on all four sides. Serious, textured, purposeful and richly symbol-filled, the soaring design is also appropriate and functional, for Chicagoans have always taken politics seriously. Ultimately this is what the drama of this neo-classical temple bespeaks. Monumental classicism fits the measure of the "people's palace" that the City of Chicago and the government of Cook County share and have sought to build. In addition, they would require a structure that would also be in the truest modern sense an efficient office building. Grandeur and efficiency were together wed in this bold design. Shortly after the new structure opened, an architectural critic wrote –

In "scale" the (Corinthian) order exceeds anything west of Albany...This would, of itself, make a building noteworthy anywhere, but it is also to be said that it has been well and faithfully studied in mass, in scale, and in detail. It is not only much the most impressive thing of its kind that Chicago has to show, but one of the most impressive in the United States, and in the interior...there is not only a faithful study of style, but features which show an escape from the style into the vigor of individual invention, and a richness which has even elements of novelty in decorative effect.

City Hall is the home of Chicago's municipal government. Here the Executive Branch, formed by the mayor and the commissioners of various departments, and the Legislative Branch, made up of the fifty elected aldermen from the City's fifty wards, and the City Council's committees, conduct the affairs of the metropolis that has been termed the "Capital of the American Heartland." The historic City Council Chamber located on the building's second floor is home to the legislative assembly in which municipal laws are enacted according to the authority granted by the Illinois Constitution's "Home Rule" provision. The building is by necessity shaped by its function. The business of this municipal

edifice is chiefly concerned with the shaping of urban law and the delivery of municipal services to the neighborhoods of the City. Over the course of the last 100 years of its existence, Chicago's City Hall has experienced an evolving sense of practical functionality. With more than 1,200 workers on the City Hall side of the building alone, the sheer volume of employees and city department offices has continuously reshaped the interior contours of the building's everyday life. Over the course of time some City offices and their staffs have been established in other nearby office buildings. Most City services and departments utilized by the public, however, are all contained within the eleven floors of the present governmental headquarters along LaSalle Street.

This structure is the City's seventh City Hall, brought to life between 1908 and 1911 on a piece of sacred space—one that has long endured as the home of all things political on the corner of Randolph and LaSalle Streets. Remarkably, this structure and two of its predecessors at this very same site all have endured as joint ventures between the governments of the City of Chicago and Cook County. Since 1853 the City and the County have shared a common home, co-existing side-by-side, two curious tectonic plates riding the political fortunes that have grown up so demonstrably here. No other municipal building in the City's past, however, has possessed the monumental, robust character that this one does.

And yet, the six other City Halls that have graced the landscape of Chicago since its incorporation in 1837 also have their own places in the fabric of Chicago's history, having accompanied the City through its ascendancy into one of the world's premier cities. This book is the story of these edifices, their history, their architecture and the significance each building has played in the City's development.

In telling the tale of the physicality of the City Hall buildings throughout Chicago's history, a secondary narrative must be told, a history of some of the extraordinary men and women who designed, occupied and gave life to these buildings and, as a result, their city. Mayors, aldermen, City employees and architects have invested themselves in monumentalizing the City's political ethos for over 150 years. Without them, no amount of wood and stone could take on such significance and relevance. As Winston Churchill said –

We shape our buildings; thereafter they shape us.

It is our hope that this book can remind us how Chicagoans have shaped their City Hall buildings and how they, in turn, will continue to shape us as well.

Chicago was incorporated as a town in 1833 and as a city in 1837. It left its fur-trading outpost character quickly in the dust. From then until the turn of the century it was the fastest growing city on the planet earth. What was the secret of such fast-paced success? It was our location, location, location—at the geographical juncture where the prairie meets the Great Lakes. The waterways of the nation all connect, the Native American peoples knew, through this spot at the southern tip of Lake Michigan.

During the 19th Century our central location in the heart of the nation made us a destination for people on the move. Transplanted Americans and vast numbers of immigrants made their way to Chicago for a fresh start. It is in that energy and mayhem where our book begins.

No other city in the nation experienced the remarkable boom in population that Chicago did as it began. When the little trading post incorporated as a town in 1833 and as a city, four years later, in 1837, there were only 4,000 residents. In just 13 years, by 1850, there were 29,000. Remarkably, over the next ten years, the population went on to triple in numbers to 112,000. And by 1870, there were almost 300,000 living in Chicago. Urban growth was being redefined in Chicago. This 300,000 was the population on October 8, 1871, when after the driest fall on record, the greatest calamity in the City's history struck.

The fire that rained over the City was unlike anything anyone had ever seen. Fanned by exceptionally powerful prairie winds, funnels of fire gyrated over the City, street by street. Before it, intense walls of heat vanquished everything in its path. Buildings did not so much catch on fire, as you might expect, rather they more or less exploded into flame block-by-block and house-by-house. When the fire reached the Chicago River, it leapt across, undaunted by the width of the water.

Nothing could survive the onslaught of the inferno. Leveled in its path were the City Hall, the Court House, the commodity exchanges, the City's premier churches, the Roman Catholic cathedral, the Episcopal cathedral, many hotels (Potter Palmer's newest was only open for three weeks), as well as schools, colleges, homes, bank after bank, and business after business—all reduced to ash with equal, unprejudiced ferocity. More than $200 million worth of property was destroyed. However, less than 300 people appear to have perished.

Strangely, the Great Fire ended like it began, mysteriously. After what seemed like an eternity of fire, a gentle rain fell on the evening of October 10th that helped to extinguish the flames. In the four square mile footprint of the destruction three-fifths of the City lay in ruin. But as gigantic a loss as the fire was, its size would only be surpassed by what followed—the massive rebuilding of Chicago.

As you might imagine, the Chicago that burned was a rough, disordered urban terrain. Little attention had been given in the decades of the City's rapid growth for the more structured organization of urban planning. It is fair to say that the fire carried away a host of urban mistakes. In the enormous effort to rebuild the City, many of those clumsy errors were never repeated.

The Great Fire of 1871 was a moment that reset all the City's clocks. It was a moment in which everyone could set out to begin again. 90,000 people, after all, were made homeless by the blaze. New homes, new commercial structures, new municipal buildings all required a plan of extraordinary proportions. Erased in the fury of the fire was, of course, the City Hall in which the body of Abraham Lincoln had been waked on its journey to Springfield, the State Capital in May 1865. With it most essential structures had been lost leaving the landscape barren and filled with waste. This is important to understand because this experience of devastation was at the center of Chicago life. Only in understanding the destruction was it possible to appreciate what the new structures that would soon rise really meant.

Crowd gathered to watch the cornerstone laying ceremony for the new City Hall. 1909. DN-0007525, *Chicago Daily News* negatives collection, Chicago History Museum.

Once loans to rebuild were secured, the largest in the history of America then, the massive undertaking of rebuilding commenced and out of the ashes the nation's most modern city would eventually rise. The Second City would eclipse the first. And the epic task of rebuilding the heartland capital of the nation would bring tens of thousands of new people to Chicago, eager for work and a chance to be part of an enterprise of never-before-witnessed proportions. For Chicago, the Great Fire was not only a tragedy and a disaster; it was also an unequalled opportunity to start again. In this period of recovery the true meaning of architectural significance began—an enterprise that would never cease. It was no accident that when the World's Columbian Exposition of 1893 opened some twenty-years later, many of the 27 million people who came to see the fair, really came to see the miracle that was Chicago. They were dazzled by what they found. Everyone coming to Chicago was looking for something; everyone coming to Chicago brought something with them as well.

I believe that we have been successful in helping to part the curtain of history that has covered or obscured some of Chicago's greatest developments. Nothing signaled Chicago greatness more than the massive undertakings of building design and construction that seemed to go on non-stop. No single institution has invested so much urban energy over the decades more than Chicago City government in shaping and sculpting the landscape of the City's center with the great structures of its City Halls. Displaying their designs and identifying their important impact on Chicago life has been the reason for our present efforts. Commemorating the grandeur of our City's present, and seventh, City Hall designed by the Chicago architectural firm of Holabird & Roche 100 years ago gives all Chicagoans, especially those of us who work within its walls, a great reason to celebrate.

Chicago architect Frank Lloyd Wright said— *Every spirit builds itself a house, and beyond its house, a world, and beyond its world, a heaven. Know, then, that the world exists for you. Build, therefore, your own world.*

Holabird & Roche produced a building that was a perfect fit for the enterprise of Chicago's urban government. Best of all they provided a building of powerful aesthetics that made all who entered it conscious of the important and vital work that was conducted here. It was no accident that they fashioned a neo-classical Greek Temple— romantic, imperious and emitting a sense of power and majesty of design. Chicago's political leaders went beyond the parameters of all City Hall buildings that went before. Their efforts dazzled not only Chicagoans, but set tongues wagging across the nation. The sheer scale of the building was a challenge to the tastes and refinements of the early 20th Century. In the city that had invented the skyscraper, the proportions of the bold massing of the seventh City Hall was refreshingly modern and bright.

"Architecture is the will of an epoch translated into space."
Mies van der Rohe

Introduction
By Honorable Edward M. Burke

"Architecture is music in space, as it were, a frozen music."
Friedrich Von Schelling

It is no exaggeration to say that since my election to the City Council in 1969 I have had a front row seat to view Chicago history—like it or not.

I have served in the Council with seven Chicago mayors—Richard J. Daley; Michael Bilandic; Jane Byrne; Harold Washington; David Orr; Eugene Sawyer and Richard M. Daley.

During this time I have served with some two hundred twenty-four aldermanic colleagues.

I have always believed it is important to study history, to examine it and to understand the manner in which events and institutions have come to occur. Few things are ever written in stone, especially in politics. But without the ability to comprehend the synthesis of history—how the whole thing fits together—much can be lost.

This is important particularly when, as members of the legislative branch of municipal government, we have the opportunity, on occasions, to learn from the mistakes of the past. It has been said—*To know the truth of history is to realize its ultimate myth and its inevitable ambiguity.*

When I came to the City Council forty years ago, it was largely a closed operation run by Alderman Tom Keane and a few of his closest associates. In those days it was rare that anyone he did not designate could even rise to speak on a matter. That was the way it was—they did not need any help, and did not encourage any activity. At 25 years of age, I was not about to tip over the apple cart.

Nothing much happened until the arrival of 10th Ward Alderman Ed Vrdolyak in 1971. Together, with 21st Alderman Wilson Frost, we engineered what was called the "Coffee Rebellion" in which we demanded a larger voice in the Council from Alderman Keane. We made some bold demands in that small-scaled mutiny planned at our early morning coffees at the Sherman House, the hotel at the northwest corner of Randolph and Clark Streets, across the street from City Hall. We demanded some assurances that legislation we might propose would be favorably received, as well as having access to briefing sessions in advance of Council meetings. Remarkably we actually achieved some of our demands. Things started to change.

Few Chicagoans recall today that between 1837 and 1847 members of the City Council served just one year terms. And that this was lengthened to two years in 1847. Or that from 1839 to 1922 thirty-five wards elected two aldermen each, until in 1923 when each ward was restricted to just one alderman elected for a two year term. The present system of one alderman elected for four years was only established in 1935 with the election of the 92nd City Council.

As you can see, like most things in Chicago, the Council evolved over the course of time with its history adjusting to the shape of the times.

But one thing has remained constant—the majestic structure that is our home—the Chicago City Hall. This lasting piece of heroic American architecture by the Chicago architectural firm of Holabird & Roche remains a fitting place in which to conduct the people's business. Broad, bold and muscular, there is an almost robustness to its design. For the past one hundred years the enterprise of Chicago's political life has unfolded in this transformative building. The great Chicago architect Louis Sullivan once said—*Form follows function*. These words have become a unique part of Chicago's vocabulary. But many times over the past forty years I have thought that our function just might be following the form of our governmental home. So noble is its frame; so purposeful is its aesthetic; so demanding is its character that the building itself adds civility and grandeur to the events and efforts that unfolded here for 100 years.

The Chicago architectural firm of Holabird & Roche was founded here in 1880. Since that time William Holabird and Martin Roche have helped to reshape Chicago with a long line of magnificent structures which are an intricate part of our urban story. It is no accident that they were both young architects employed with the great William LeBaron Jenney when he created the very first skyscraper in America here in Chicago (1884), the Home Insurance Building on LaSalle Street. From the Monadnock Building (1890) and the Marquette Building (1895) to Soldier Field (1924), the *Chicago Daily News* Building (1929) and the Board of Trade (1930), to name just a few, the most textured and refined architecture in our nation rose on the streets of Chicago because of Holabird & Roche. Proudly, the firm, Holabird & Root, its successor, remains in operation today. In Chicago's City Hall they demonstrate with intelligence and elegance the saying—*An architect is the drawer of dreams*

I think it is safe to say that I speak for all my colleagues in the Chicago City Council, past and present, when I say that we treasure the remarkable human achievement which shaped and designed our legislative home. We honor the craft and intelligence that helped it to rise in the canyon of LaSalle Street. And we celebrate the lofty sensibilities that brought it to life. Chicago's present, and seventh, City Hall is, of course, our most remarkable— not just because it was born in the America of invention and modern abilities, but because it has truly stood the test of time. No other Chicago City Hall has stood so long; so effective; or so majestic. While it might be the product of the Edwardian Age, it has always been able to evolve to serve the purpose and the enterprise for which it was designed—a home for municipal government in the most wondrous of modern American cities.

Mayor Richard J. Daley presides over a
Chicago City Council Meeting in the 1960s.
Courtesy Chicago History Museum

First City Hall
1837-1842

"Less is more."
Mies van der Rohe

On March 4, 1837, the City of Chicago was incorporated, a "City in a garden." The original footprint occupied less than one-half of a square mile bounded by Kinzie, Des Plaines, Madison and State Streets. In the four years since its founding as a town, Chicago's population had soared from 350 to over 4,000. The forces of geography and history had poised Chicago to become an ideal transportation hub and burgeoning financial center, one of the premier cities in the United States.

Seal of the City of Chicago designed by 1st Ward Alderman Dr. Josiah C. Goodhue (1837-1838)

The Saloon Building, Chicago's First City Hall. Photograph from A.T. Andreas' *History of Chicago*, vol. 1, 1884.

William Butler Ogden (1805-1877) was elected the City's first mayor in 1837 and quickly began transforming the City from a sleepy prairie community into a bustling metropolis. He seemed to embody the vibrant spirit of Chicago—that Prairie character of rich and abiding American "know-how."

I was born close to a saw mill, was early left an orphan, christened in a millpond, graduated at a log school house, and at fourteen fancied I could do any thing I turned my hand to, and that nothing was impossible..." (William Butler Ogden)

Ogden, along with the ten Aldermen of the first Chicago Common Council's six wards (two aldermen each from four wards, one each from the 3rd and 5th Wards until 1839), was responsible for giving shape to many aspects of the City in its infancy. Ogden is credited with maintaining an air of financial calm during the Panic of 1837 which swept the nation. He kept Chicago financially solvent and refused the let the City be caught up in the national morass that existed everywhere. Most of all he kept Chicago from falling into debt.

One of Ogden's tasks was to obtain a location where the operations of city government could take place. In May of 1837, the Common Council leased space in the Saloon Building located on the southeast corner of Clark and Lake Streets. The building, named for the hall on its third floor, was built in 1836 by George W. Dole and Captain John B. Russell. The term "saloon" as applied to this building carried with it a very different connotation of a tavern than is commonplace today.

Its usage was synonymous with the French word *salon*, meaning "grand and spacious hall." Such halls provided a forum for debate for many Enlightenment philosophers of 18th century France including Montesquieu and Voltaire. These *salons* helped foster many of the democratic ideals upon which the American political system is founded. It is fitting that the first home of Chicago's urban government and legislature should be named after the historic venues which provided

such a rich tradition in political debate as some would say laid the groundwork for its Prairie assembly.

Not everyone understood the political and philosophical nomenclature for the site. A writer would later declare that there was "eternal fitness" to the fact that Chicago's first political leaders convened in a building thus named. "It matters not that there was no bar in the edifice. Its occupancy by the Aldermen and the business calling a large number of the men who have since served on the board go to show there is something in a name."

For all of the grandeur associated with the enterprise, the City's lease in the Saloon Building covered just one room on the second floor of the multipurpose building. Both the Common Council, as the City Council was known then, and the Municipal Court conducted business there; the rest of the building was devoted to shops and stores, other offices, as well as the large "Saloon" on the upper floor. The entire building was truly a modern day Market Place—an Athenian agora—political and religious meetings, concerts, traveling shows, public markets and many other civic entertainments all took place there. In 1837, a young Stephen A. Douglas delivered an oration there which captured the hearts of Chicagoans, beginning a tradition of political debate in Chicago's City Hall.

The first City Hall was home to many politicians who played a defining role in Chicago's early years. Mayor Ogden was inventive, designing the City's first "swing bridge" over the Chicago River at Clark Street. In addition he was also instrumental in promoting the growth of both canals, a breakthrough form of transportation at that time, and railroads, just in their infancy, offering the promise of connecting Chicago's commerce and agriculture to all sectors of the country. Following Ogden's one year term as mayor, he remained active in Chicago's political life. He was elected the alderman of the 6th Ward in 1840 and alderman of the 9th Ward in 1847.

William Butler Ogden,
1st Mayor (1837-1838)

Buckner Stith Morris,
2nd Mayor (1838-1839)

Benjamin Wright Raymond,
3rd and 6th Mayor
(1839-1840, 1842-1843)

Alexander Loyd,
4th Mayor (1840-1841)

During this period of the first City Hall one of the City's most enduring institutions also came to life. In 1837, Francis Cornwall Sherman, Chicago's fifth and 23rd mayor (1841-1842, 1862-1865), opened the City Hotel, renamed the Sherman House in 1844. It was the first four-story building in the City. The hotel would occupy a pre-eminent place in the political life of Chicago for 138 years as the meeting ground for political intrigues and lunch spot for hungry politicians.

Several notable aldermen also shaped the City's fortunes during this period of the first City Hall through their ingenuity and hard work. Josiah Goodhue (1st Ward, 1837-1838) designed the City's first seal and helped create a public school system. George W. Dole (6th Ward, 1838-1839), was responsible for building the Saloon Building, and is credited as being the father of Chicago's meatpacking industry, a business that would later come to dominate Chicago commerce for over a century. Dole was also Chairman of the Committee on Finance from 1838-1839 and 1842-1844.

John H. Kinzie (6th Ward, 1839-1840), the son of Chicago's first white settlers, also served as the Chairman of the Finance Committee and earlier served as second President of Chicago in 1834, before the City was incorporated. His wife, Juliette, published a firsthand account of the historic Fort Dearborn Massacre, when over 60 people were killed and the early Chicago settlement of Fort Dearborn was burned to the ground by Pottawatomie warriors in league with the British during the War of 1812.

Politicians like Ogden, Kinzie and Sherman nurtured the City of Chicago in its first years and established a foundation for bigger and better things to come. Although Chicago politics literally began in a one room operation, the Saloon, at Clark and Lake Streets, the need for the physical expansion of government offices would quickly become apparent to all. Chicagoans were fashioned from a true pioneer spirit at this time. They were inventive, resilient and pragmatic. Their first City Hall was reflective of their Prairie character - simple, effective and unpretentious.

The remains of Fort Dearborn. Courtesy, Chicago History Museum

Bird's-eye view of Chicago, 1860. Courtesy, Chicago History Museum

The First Cook County Building built at the southwest corner of Clark and Randolph Streets in 1835. Courthouse on main floor and Cook County business in the basement, with old Fort Dearborn in the rear. Photograph from *America's City Halls*.

Second City Hall
1842-1848

"We shape our buildings: thereafter they shape us."
Winston Churchill

With the City's five year lease soon expiring on the
Saloon Building in 1841, plans were developed to
purchase the first government-owned building for the
City of Chicago. The City demonstrated healthy signs
of growth as the population rose to 4,470, and it
was fitting that it have a municipal building capable
of managing things in this period of rapid urban
expansion. When the lease on the Saloon building
did run out, Chicago's City Hall was temporarily
moved to a two-story building owned by Mrs. Nancy
Chapman at the northeast corner of Randolph and
LaSalle Streets, just across the street from the present
City Hall. The business of the City government was
conducted here from 1842 to 1848 during the period
of construction of Market Hall, the first government-
built structure exclusively for municipal use. In 1846
Chicago's population rose to some 14,000.

THE WIDOW CHAPMANS BUILDING
2ND CITY HALL.

The structure that was selected as the center of municipal government was as primitive as the frontier patina of Chicago itself. It was a two-story wood framed building with an outside stairway that rose up to the second floor. It was adequate but hardly fancy; rough and ready, a natural characteristic of local life. City Hall would remain here for the next six years. Money was tight and hard to come by for the primitive municipality. In 1842, the man who orchestrated the sale of Old Fort Dearborn to the City, Benjamin Wright Raymond, was elected Chicago's 3rd Mayor.

This was a time when the City was deeply in debt and real-estate was comparatively valueless. By a rigid course of economy [Raymond] succeeded in reducing city expenditures to about $9,800 and by the last part of the year city scrip was sold at par. (*Chicago Daily Tribune* Obituary, April 6, 1883)

By 1848, Cyrus Hall McCormick, the inventor of the Reaper, moved to Chicago and established his factory here, helping to strengthen the essential economic foundation to fashion the City into a regional, and possibly a national power. That year both a grain exchange and a livestock market opened in the City. Though in their most primitive forms, these would become the essential components of Chicago's mercantile life—the Chicago Board of Trade and the Union Stockyards.

The Common Council found itself leading a metropolis that was very different from the one they led when the City Hall was housed in the Saloon Building.

The construction of Illinois and Michigan Canal, the creation of the City's first railroad and the establishment of Chicago's first telegraph connection brought in a new era for the City's expanding population which was approaching 20,000 residents. The Canal, which had been under construction for twelve years, was a remarkable success and was critical in Chicago's growth, allowing water-transportation-access from the Great Lakes to the Mississippi River and the Gulf of Mexico. It altered the commercial distribution of goods and commodities throughout the Midwest.

The telegraph connection, originally from Chicago to Milwaukee, soon evolved into a nationwide network, connecting Chicago to the major eastern cities and their business markets. Though the new railroad was not very extensive, running only ten miles west of the city, it marked a new day in urban Chicago, just as the Common Council moved to relocate to their new home. Within the decade, however, it would expand to such a point that Chicago would become the railway hub of the entire nation, assisting in the influx of Irish, German and other European immigrants who soon became the very face of the City, influencing its politics and culture.

Mayor Augustus Garrett
7th Mayor (1843–1844)
9th Mayor (1845–1846)

Mayor Alson S. Sherman,
8th Mayor (1844-1845)

Mayor John Putnam Chapin
10th Mayor (1846–1847)

Photographs of former Chicago Mayors John Blake Rice, 24th Mayor (1865-1867, 1867-1869) and Roswell B. Mason, 25th Mayor (1869-1871), 1914. DN-0063407, *Chicago Daily News* negatives collection, Chicago History Museum.

Photographs of former Chicago Mayors Thomas Dyer, 18th Mayor (1856-1857), John Wentworth, 19th and 21st Mayor (1857-1858, 1860-1861) and John Charles Haines, 20th Mayor (1858-1859, 1859-1860) 1914. DN-0063401, *Chicago Daily News* negatives collection, Chicago History Museum.

Photograph of former Chicago Mayors Isaac Lawrence Milliken, 16th Mayor (1854-1855), Levi D. Boone, 17th Mayor (1855-1856) and Thomas Dyer, 18th Mayor (1856-1857), 1914. DN-0063403, *Chicago Daily News* negatives collection, Chicago History Museum.

Photographs of former Chicago Mayors Joseph Medill, 26th Mayor (1871-1873) and Harvey Doolittle Colvin, 27th Mayor (1873-1875) 1914. DN-0063411, *Chicago Daily News* negatives collection, Chicago History Museum.

Third City Hall
1848-1853

Make no little plans. They have no magic to stir men's blood and probably themselves will not be realized. Make big plans. Aim high in hope and work. Remembering that a noble, logical diagram once recorded will not die."
Daniel Hudson Burnham

The 1840s found Chicago, even in the earliest days of its life as a city, experiencing a swift growth. In the decade between 1840 and 1850 the urban population grew from 4,470 to 29,963, expanding more than five times. Twenty-percent of the population had been born in Ireland immigrating during the era of the Great Hunger. Some came to Chicago during the epoch in which the Illinois and Michigan Canal had been built, digging their way to a new life in the City inch-by-inch and mile-by-mile along the 90-mile corridor of hand-dug waterway that linked the Illinois River to the Great Michigan Lake.

Chicago's Third City Hall on State Street
between Randolph and Washington Streets.
Photograph from *America's City Hall*

For Chicago's municipal government, Nancy Chapman's two-story frame building which served as the City Hall at the northeast corner of LaSalle and Randolph Streets was far too constraining for its needs and sense of its own destiny. It was a City on the move, filled with an understanding of its own potential and power. Commerce and industry were expanding and the municipal character of Chicago was unfolding in unexpected ways. The meager proportions of their "saloon" City Hall were no longer physically or emotionally able to embody their vision of themselves. The massive undertaking of the Illinois and Michigan Canal project had given everyone a vital understanding of what Chicago was capable of accomplishing. They had large plans for the future. On April 3, 1848, the Chicago Board of Trade, a staple of Chicago's mercantile life, opened and demonstrated a robust financial muscularity for the City.

Nothing evidenced progress more than the construction of Chicago's first railroad depot, though modest by the standards which were soon to follow. The Galena and Chicago Union Railroad built its first depot at the southwest corner of Canal and Kinzie Streets. In 1848 the introduction of a full scale telegraph system connected Chicago to the east coast. That same year, chloroform was used for the first time in a medical procedure in Chicago, though it would be 1852 before the City's first hospital, Mercy Hospital, actually opened. During the mid-1840s six hundred new buildings a year were being constructed; the City learned how to finance and implement large scale public improvements. All this gave Chicago a strong sense of the newness and freshness of the world around it—filled with invention and an unbridled sense of the future. It also gave Chicagoans a sense that the effects of the Great Financial Panic of 1847 were on the wane and more exciting times were ahead. More than ever Chicago needed a municipal governmental center worthy of the City's potential.

A plan was developed to construct a new City Hall, known as Market Hall, along State Street between Randolph and Lake Streets, the first government-owned building built specifically for municipal use. Architect John Mills Van Osdel, founder of the first architectural firm in Chicago (1844), was commissioned by the Common Council to design the $11,070 structure on a 40 foot by 80 foot piece of land. The two-story complex he envisioned combined a City Hall with a public market on the ground floor to be constructed of brick and stone with an accompanying tower.

A Chicago Journal Editorial informed Chicago residents that the project for a new City Hall was moving along right on schedule— *We have been shown a drawing by Van Osdel for a City Market, which will, if built in accordance with the design shown us, be a decided ornament to the city while it will remedy an evil long complained of by our citizens. It is contemplated to erect this, the first of a series, in the center of State Street between Randolph and Lake. It is to be built of brick 80 feet long and 40 wide—to be two stories high, to contain 32 stalls, and will cost from 8 to $10,000. The Committee on Finance reported in favor of the project at the last meeting of the Common Council, and Geo. Smith & Co. with others, offered to loan the city sufficient funds to build it. We are glad to see the matter progress so far, and hope to announce the commencement of preparations for erecting this market at no very distant day.* (*Chicago Journal,* November 9, 1847)

On November 13, 1848, members of the Common Council occupied their Chambers on the second floor of the Market Hall for the first time. The ground floor was leased out to farmers and other merchants in a series of commercial stalls opened to the public. Combining a space for municipal government and a public market was a clever way to recover costs of construction in the nineteenth century. John Van Osdel divided the outer part of the first floor into 32 stalls easily accessible for the marketing of produce, leaving the interior rooms accessible for City use. In addition to creating the Council Chambers on the second floor, Van Osdel provided the City with a library and an office for the City Clerk. Mayors during the era of the Market Hall included:

Mayor James Curtis
11th Mayor (1847–1848)
13th Mayor (1850–1851

Mayor Walter S. Gurnee
14th Mayor (1851–1853)

James Curtis (1847-1848 & 1850-1851), James Hutchinson Woodworth (1848-1850), Walter S. Gurnee (1851-1853) and Charles McNeill Gray (1853-1854).

It was in the Chambers of the Common Council during this era that a spectacular debate was witnessed regarding the rights of American citizens. With the passage of the Fugitive Slave Act in September of 1850, requiring assistance from Northern states in the capture and return of fugitive slaves, the Chicago Common Council expressed its reluctance to accept the Act as law. The Chicago press was unusually consistent in its denunciation of the Act, placing pressure on Mayor James Curtis and the aldermen of the nine wards. In an October meeting, the Council considered Alderman Amos G. Throop's proposed resolution officially condemning the Act, insisting that it violated the constitutional rights of all men, and therefore could not be legally binding.

The resolution went on to admonish Senators and Congressmen of Free States who failed in their duties by allowing the Act to pass, comparing them to traitors such as Benedict Arnold and Judas Iscariot. The resolution was adopted, making clear that the Council had no plans to require City authorities or citizens in general, to actively assist in the capture of run-away slaves from the South. The subject was opened for debate to allow the Council to gauge public opinion. They listened to arguments from both sides. Senator Stephen A. Douglas (Democrat, Illinois) spoke in defense of the Act for the first time in a Free State, questioning the authority of the Common Council of Chicago to nullify Acts of Congress. He insisted that the Act did not suspend *habeas corpus* and the right to trial, while also disputing comparisons of historical traitors to himself and his colleagues. The Council repealed their nullifying resolution the following day.

NORTH FRONT OF 1ST STRUCTURE ERECTED BY CITY FOR CITY PURPOSES. KNOWN AS THE MARKET BUILDING

The front of the Market Building. *Chicago Tribune* photo archive, October 2, 1898.

Chicago architect John M. Van Osdell, the designer of two Chicago City Halls, the 4th and 6th. Chicago History Museum.

Fourth City Hall
1853-1871

"Architecture exhibits the greatest extent of the difference from nature which may exist in works of art. It involves all the powers of design, and is sculpture and painting inclusively. It shows the greatness of man, and should at the same time teach him humility."
Samuel Taylor Coleridge

During the decades when this venerable municipal building stood with open doors in what Chicagoans called "Court-House" Square, the area bordered by Clark, LaSalle, Washington and Randolph Streets, Chicago continued to soar in commerce, industry and population. When the building opened in 1853 Chicago boasted of a population of some 30,000. By 1860, the year the City hosted its very first national presidential political convention— the Republican Convention of 1860—in which favorite son, Abraham Lincoln, received the Republican Party's nomination for the Presidency— the population had surpassed 100,000; an increase that expanded the population by more than three times.

By the eve of the Great Fire which would level the beloved City-Hall/County Courthouse complex, the population of Chicago was just under 300,000. These staggering statistics are an indication of the unprecedented growth which was taking place. All areas of urban life were expanding—industry, finance, housing, immigration, migration from other parts of the nation, commerce, religion and politics. The ever-expanding municipality of Chicago was a city where commercial giants were reinventing how Americans lived. It was a natural outgrowth of this expansion that the details and responsibilities of municipal and county government were enlarged every day.

By 1853 the Common Council was faced with the dilemma that it was in desperate need of further room to grow to house the government officials of the rapidly-growing municipality. At the same time, the County had outgrown its old courthouse and was experiencing similar problems. Cook County held title to the public square bounded by Washington, LaSalle, Clark and Randolph Streets which it was granted when the County was established in 1831. The County also owed the City $30,000 for various services rendered. To settle this debt, the City of Chicago and Cook County established a partnership in which the County granted the City half of the public square to construct a new City Hall. The City then gave permission to the County to obtain land on which to build a new criminal court and county hospital. The County agreed to pay three-fourths of the $111,000 construction cost of the new complex jointly occupied by the City and County governments.

John Van Osdel was once again selected as the architect for this project. The new building, completed in 1853, was grandiose in stature, two stories in height, surmounted by two domes and a cupola, and constructed of buff limestone from the Lockport quarries. The basement housed a jail, living quarters for the jailer, the City Watch House and the Cook County Sheriff's Office. The first floor contained most of the municipal offices with an armory in the east wing of the building. The second floor was home to the Common Council

Chambers, but this soon proved to be too small and renovations adding a third story were completed in 1858. There were further renovations in 1869 due to a roof collapse in the east wing. Investigators later determined that "the roof and other portions of the building had been constructed without blueprints or architectural plans."

The *Chicago Tribune* provided a close-up look at the new Council Chambers on February 15, 1853, raising a few critical concerns.

The new Council room, or rather Hall, is now nearly complete, the carpet is laid, next desks, and congress pedestal chairs are provided for each Alderman, and for the public officers; the mayor's position is on an elevated platform; in the center of the room is a large circular table for documents, and the whole is enclosed with a massive wood rail, similar to that in the Court of Common Pleas. Seats are provided for the public, but we imagine that they will be of little use, for there is no prospect of any but a stentorian orator, every being heard. As yet we have no provision for the press. Is there to be any? Or does the Council wish their proceedings to be neither overheard by the public nor seen through the press, except as prepared for the Democrat [newspaper]? The whole is ludicrously too large, and it is to be feared, from the utter neglect of the laws of sound and its construction, it will be of little use.

In 1858 a third floor was added to the City Hall/County Building complex by architect John Mills Van Osdel. It marked a harmonious addition to the busy matters of urban and county government. By late November the finishing touches were being made to the expanded enlargement. The Chamber of the Common Council was outfitted with a handsome carpet. On the new third floor the County Surveyor, the City Surveyor and the City Superintendent all occupied "commodious" office space. The City's 20th Mayor—John Charles Haines—had offices located on the second floor. He was said to be "well-accommodated."

The *Chicago Tribune* provided a detailed description of the newly refurbished structure, but had concerns over strange smells. *The building has been handsomely painted throughout, and is*

Mayor Charles McNeill Gray 15th Mayor (1853-1854)

Mayor Roswell B. Mason, (1869-1871) Chicago's 25th chief executive when the Great Fire began. Chicago History Museum, CHi31917.

Chicago's 17th Mayor, Levi Boone, (1855-1856) a descendant of Daniel Boone. Chicago Public Library Archive.

The body of slain President Abraham Lincoln arrives
in Chicago on its way to lay-in-state in the City Hall-County
Building, May 1, 1865. Chicago History Museum, i22122.

Chicagoans throng to the City Hall-Courthouse building for President Lincoln's laying-in-state. Chicago History Museum, i11258aa.

warmed by steam. In this latter respect, we believe some one has blundered in giving the steam pipes throughout the building a coat of paint. This would do well enough for summer fashions, as it looks pretty; but from the heated surface as painted is constantly emitted a sickening and unpleasant, and doubtless unhealthy odor. The heat will not be sufficient to destroy the paint and thus gradually diminish the evil, which will most likely be a permanent one for some winters to come. (November 29, 1858)

The addition to the government complex demonstrated the growing amount of work that government faced as the City prospered and grew. Mayor Francis C. Sherman summed up Chicago's remarkable success in his May 5, 1862 inaugural address, providing an accurate image of the City's urban character. *Allow me to congratulate you that notwithstanding the general disturbance of financial and business relations, the enterprise, capital, and resources of Chicago have secured us to a great extent from the misfortunes that have befallen other cities. Our trade and manufactories are increasing with wonderful rapidity, real estates is saleable at improving prices, new buildings are projected and being built in great numbers, and with proper attention to our interests, we may hope before many years to take the front rank among the great cities of this continent.*

Another expansion was soon to come with the addition of east and west wings to the structure in 1869. The expansion precluded the unpopular notion that an entire new City Hall complex needed to be constructed. Municipal employees had been moved to other locations to effectively deal with over-crowding conditions. However storage space for important public records was making big demands on the building's space, being placed outside of the safety of the City's vault areas. Fears that important documents could be lost heightened the need for more space. *The loss of public records would result in endless litigation, and another season should not be allowed to pass over without some provision for the safety of the books*—the *Chicago Tribune* said. They went on to point out—*The city is now paying very*

high rents for comparatively indifferent apartments for several branches of the city government, and with the indifferent accommodations for any of the city offices. There is not a book or a record of the city that in case of fire can be reasonably expected to be saved. (*Chicago Tribune*, March 14, 1868)

Despite the need for a new City Hall, constructing one which would necessitate a large debt for the City was out of the question and politically unpopular. But these were not the only cautions preventing construction. Many believed that a new City Hall would carry Chicago into the 20th century and would need to reflect a new spirit of architectural excellence. *When the city builds a new City Hall, it should be with a view of answering public uses for at least half a century. Is the city prepared now to decide upon a site that will be convenient for the next fifty years?* (*Chicago Tribune*, December 11, 1867)

An important transition occurred in Chicago's municipal government on March 10, 1869. The City was reconfigured from ten to twenty wards expanding to meet the ever widening needs of the population. A change occured in the date of Municipal elections, moving them from April to November.

The fourth City Hall witnessed some very influential politicians during its time. Charles Gray (1853-1854) was the mayor at the time the fourth City Hall was built. There were also other notable mayors such as Levi Day Boone (1855-1856), the great-nephew of Daniel Boone, who established the Chicago's first police force. Mayor Thomas Dyer (1856-1857) was the founding President of the Chicago Board of Trade, an iconic business market still is flourishing today. Mayor John "Long John" Wentworth (1857-1858, 1860-1861) may have been the tallest mayor in Chicago's history at 6' 6," but he also was responsible for President Abraham Lincoln's nomination at the 1860 Republican National Convention in Chicago. General Ulysses S. Grant was nominated for the Presidency at the 1868 Republican National Convention in Chicago during John Rice's term as mayor (1865-1867, 1867-1869). Aside from the long list of powerful mayors, the fourth City Hall saw its fair share of notable alderman. John Comiskey (1863-1865, 1867-1869) served as the alderman of the seventh and

Mayor Julian Rumsey
22nd Mayor (1861–1862),
nephew of 6th Ward Alderman
George Washington Dole.

A drawing shows the 1858 addition of a third story to the building. Photograph from *America's City Halls*.

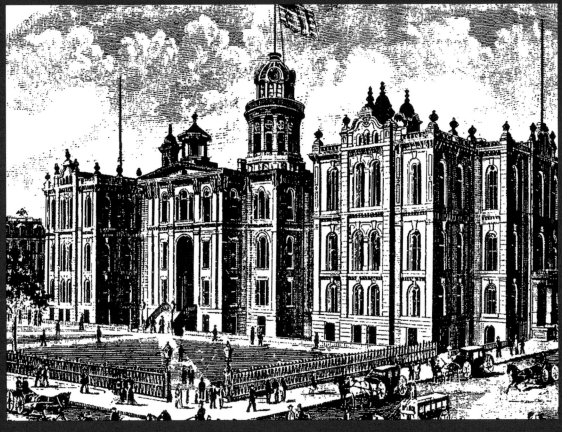

In 1859, two wings were added to the east and west sides of the building. This is the City Hall that burned in 1871. Photograph from *America's City Halls*.

eighth wards. He was the first President of the Chicago Board of Aldermen and also served as the Chairman of the Committee on Finance from 1862-1865. His son, Charles, founded the Chicago White Sox.

On October 8, 1871 the massive, 10,000 pound bell of City Hall sounded the alarm for its citizens as the fury of Prairie winds drove a fire across the face of the City. Chicago had endured an unseasonably hot and dry summer and fall which left the wooden planked City a tinder box of danger. More than two dozen fires had broken out over the previous few weeks leaving the geography of Chicago spotted with the charred remains of smaller, isolated, controllable fires. But when the watchman caught sight of the spire of smoke burning at the southwest edge of the City, at Clinton and DeKoven Streets, near 12th Street (Roosevelt Road), he also glimpsed what was left of the City's heavily damaged fire equipment returning from a large fire which had burned since the previous day. Fire equipment had not even had a chance to return to their fire houses when the signs of another and more deadly fire became evident. Events which transformed this particular fire into the single largest disaster in Chicago history were the powerful winds which began to pick up and fan the inferno like none before. Gyres, or pillars of intense heat, began to grow and move ahead of the actual flames. Houses did not so much "catch fire" as they simply exploded from the extreme heat. There was little that could prevent the power of the fire from moving north and east of the Chicago River's south branch. Many believed the destruction would be stopped at the river's edge in the downtown area. However, no one could have predicted the power which drove the cataclysm and allowed it to pass over and leap over the river. Before the flames would be extinguished, the fire burned its way up to Fullerton Avenue three miles beyond the north bank of the river. Three-fifths of the central business district would be wiped out. Nearly everything in the path of the fire would be erased, save for a few structures, most notably the Water Tower (the stand pipe for the pumping station at what today is Michigan and Chicago Avenues) and the house of Maylon Ogden, brother of Chicago's first mayor, William B. Ogden.

Today the site is home to Newberry Library at Dearborn and Walton Streets. But the devastation was acute and Chicago's most important buildings perished in what would become known as the Great Chicago Fire.

Courthouse Square housing both the Fourth City Hall and the Cook County Courthouse was gone. It had stood for eighteen years, but was short-lived with the conflagration easily consuming the building. Some three hundred citizens of Chicago perished in the fire, with another 90,000 left homeless. In order to ensure the continuity of local government, the Common Council established a temporary City Hall on the second floor of a building at the intersection of Ashland Avenue and Washington Streets on the westside in the First Congregational Church where Mary Todd Lincoln once worshipped. While the City was still smoldering, a committee appointed by the Council selected the West Madison Street police station as a temporary home for the Council's business. This police station would continue to function as the seat of local government for the next two months until a new City Hall was constructed.

Two months after the fire, Joseph Medill, the long-time owner-publisher of the *Chicago Tribune* was elected mayor on the "Fire-Proof" ticket. His words outline the actual cost of all that had been lost. He gave the disaster a sober analysis, but his words also reflected the hope that filled the Chicago air. He echoed the sentiments of Chicagoans who were set on rebuilding a new Chicago—a Second City. *All these burnt structures, machines, bridges, sidewalks, fixtures, and furniture must be rebuilt and replaced at the earliest practicable moment, as they are indispensable to the city and citizens.* (Inaugural Address, December 4, 1871)

Medill was the City's 26th Mayor. His election was a response on the part of Chicago voters to change the political structure and go outside the channels of regular political life to find someone of high ability and commercial sense to help bring the City back to life. Medill was a plain-spoken realist. From the very beginning he presented voters with a fair and reliable understanding of what they had lost. He catalogued the specifics of what had been destroyed.

But the destruction of this property is not the only loss suffered by the corporation. The burning of records, vouchers, books, papers, tax warrants, assessment rolls, etc., will necessarily occasion much loss, confusion, and embarrassment to the City Government. But it is believed that a large part of the apparent loss of official knowledge and data can be supplied from other sources. Still the pecuniary loss to the city will be considerable in the destruction of the evidence of delinquent taxes and special assessments. Medill itemized the physical loss in the fire to the city's government.

The books and papers destroyed, or saved, are reported to me as follows:

Mayor's Office—Everything in the Mayor's office was destroyed by the fire, but no public records or documents were kept there.

City Comptroller's Office—All the records, books, papers, and files of the Comptroller's office, from its commencement down to the date of the fire, are destroyed. Fortunately for the city, the charter has, since 1857, required the Comptroller to publish an annual statement of receipts and expenditures and liabilities of the city, and, since 1861, to publish a monthly statement of receipts and expenditures. From the published proceedings of the Common Council, all of which are obtainable, the general financial condition of the city up to September 1, 1871, can be ascertained. The September statement, which was prepared and ready for publication, was burnt.

City Clerk's Office—Only the books, proceedings, and documents destroyed after the 15th of September. All documents previous to that time in the vault are preserved in good condition, which is very fortunate, as they are of more value to the city than all the books and papers that were lost.

City Treasurer's Office—All books and vouchers in his hands destroyed; but the public moneys were deposited in bank vaults and are safe.

Tax Commissioner's Office—All of the real estate assessment books for the year 1871, and all of the schedules of personal property are saved or restored. Also seventeen volumes of maps of the South and North Divisions; also thirteen volumes of maps in blank; all of the schedules of property as described and assessed from 1837 to 1871 inclusive are saved. All other records of this office were destroyed.

City Collector's Office—All the special assessment rolls and books, the general tax warrants of 1868, 1869, and 1870, and the personal property tax, uncollected from the years 1863 to 1870, inclusive; also, all other books, memoranda, &c., were destroyed. The Collector also reports the loss of "some ten thousand dollars in money, bank checks, orders on Treasurer, besides receipts, reports, and many other documents, the value of which it would be difficult to estimate.

Board of Public Works—Saved all books, vouchers, &c., belonging to the bookkeeper's department, and also the principal books of the special assessment department; all other books and memoranda were destroyed.

Board of Police and Fire—All books, records, and memoranda of this department are blotted out.

Health Department—The loss of books and papers complete.

Police Court (South Division)—All the books and dockets destroyed.

Police Court (West Division)—The books, dockets, &c., remain intact, not having been in the fire.

Police Court (North Division)—All the books and dockets destroyed.

Board of Education—All books, records, and documents destroyed, except record of the proceedings of the Board.

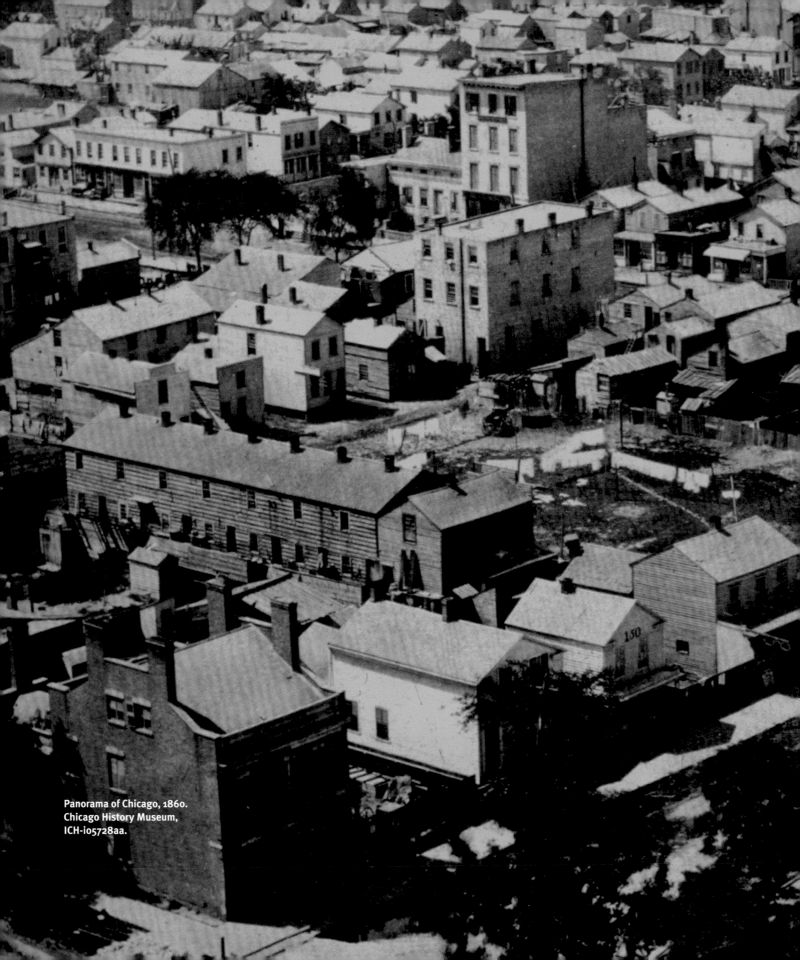

Panorama of Chicago, 1860.
Chicago History Museum,
ICH-io5728aa.

Chicagoans flee the flames over the Randolph Street Bridge, by John Chapin, Harper's Weekly. Chicago History Museum Photo Archive

A 1911 drawing by Edgar S. Cameron shows the Great Fire ravaging the Courthouse Building. DN-0009361, *Chicago Daily News* Collection, Chicago History Museum.

But I found it impossible to discuss the extraordinary condition of things in which the fire has placed the City Government in the brief space usually occupied by a Mayor's inaugural. In concluding I point with pride and admiration to the gigantic efforts our whole people are putting forth to rise from the ruins, and rebuild Chicago. The money value of their losses can hardly be calculated. But who can compute the aggregate of anguish, distress, and suffering they have endured and must yet endure? These wounds are still sore and agonizing, though they have been greatly alleviated by the prompt, generous, and world-wide charities that have been poured out for their succor and relief; and I claim in their behalf that they are showing themselves worthy the benefactions received. They have faced their calamity with noble fortitude and unflinching courage. Repining or lamentation is unheard in our midst, but hope and cheerfulness are everywhere exhibited and expressed. All are inspired with an ambition to prove to the world that they are worthy of its sympathy, confidence and assistance, and to show how bravely they can encounter disaster, how quickly repair losses, and restore Chicago to her high rank among the great cities of the earth.

Happily there is that left which fire cannot consume;—habits of industry and self-reliance, personal integrity, business aptitude, mechanical skill, and unconquerable will. These created what the flames devoured, and these can speedily recreate more than was swept away. Under free institutions, good government, and the blessings of Providence, all losses will soon be repaired, all misery caused by the fire assuaged, and a prosperity greater than ever dreamt of will be achieved in a period so brief, that the rise will astonish mankind even more than the fall of Chicago.

(Medill, Inaugural Address December 4, 1871.)

Despite the severity of the loss, Medill presented Chicagoans with some real hope. He was cautious and enlivening. He had lost as much, if not more than anyone; the Tribune Building was in ruins, though it could be rebuilt; but he was ready for the task and capable of bringing others along with him in the recovery. He was the right man at the right time.

Chicago City Hall in ruins after the Great Fire. ICH-i26548, Chicago History Museum Photo Archive.

Fifth City Hall
1872-1885

"Architecture is the learned game, correct and magnificent, of forms assembled in the light.
Le Corbusier

Mayor Joseph Medill, the long-time owner and publisher of the *Chicago Tribune*, was elected Mayor of Chicago in the aftermath of the Great Fire of 1871. It is fair to say that his popularity at the polls was a direct reaction to people's criticism of Chicago political leaders in the wake of the loss of so much of the City. People were fed up with "business as usual," and electing the taciturn Canadian-born Medill was just the medicine Chicago needed. He very tersely summed up the widespread destruction which the fire unleashed that October. His November election on the "Fire Proof Party" ticket as Chicago's 26th mayor provided him with an opportunity to remind Chicagoans what they had suffered.

In a single night and day 125,000 of our people were expelled from their homes and compelled to flee for their lives into the streets, commons, or lake, to avoid perishing in the flames. Many lost their lives from heat, suffocation, or falling walls—how many may never be known; and the multitudes who escaped were fain to seek shelter and food at the hand of charity. The greater part of our citizens, not burned out of their homes, lost their stores, shops, offices, stocks of goods, implements, books, accounts, papers, vouchers, business, or situations, and it is difficult to find any citizen who has not suffered directly by that fearful conflagration. (Inauguration Address, December 4, 1871)

One week following the fire plans were already underway for the quick construction of a new City Hall. The Common Council had passed an order calling for a structure to be built at Court-House Square, but the Board of Public Works found the site unsuitable for a new structure. Instead they went to a site further south on LaSalle Street that had been used as a water reservoir. It was constructed in less than sixty days.

In the building provision has been made for both the City and County Governments, and all will agree that the disposition of the room has been most skillful and judicious. Four separate entrances have been provided, two on Adams Street, one on LaSalle, and one on Quincy Street, so that parties having business with the various departments can reach them directly and conveniently. The principal city officers on the ground floor, all of them communicating with the fire proof vaults, which have been ingeniously and economically carved out of the old water reservoir. These vaults have walls three feet think, of solid masonry, and are much safer than those in the old Court House. There are also, on the ground floor, unassigned rooms, which the County will probably be glad to occupy, these also connecting with the vaults.

Upstairs is the Council Chamber, a large, pleasant, well-lighted room, 45 x 65 feet, with adjoining committee room. It is designed to partition off a portion of the chamber for the use of some one of the courts, as there is plenty of room to spare. On the same floor are numerous rooms for County use,

and the area will be largely increased in the spring, when the entire building will run to a height of two stories. (*Chicago Tribune*, December 19, 1871)

On January 1, 1872, the fifth City Hall opened its doors. This was an important juncture in Chicago history for the construction of a workable and reliable structure for the purposes of municipal government was a stabilizing moment in the midst of all the destruction and chaos that had gone before. It demonstrated to everyone that Chicago had the ability to rise again. Its government was open for business. It appeared capable, reliable and engaged in the task of helping life to continue. This post-fire City Hall was built as a temporary structure; but the choice of this location, in a city water cistern or reservoir, appeared to be an indication that people understood fire as a serious consequence of urban life. There was a peculiar caution in the air. Construction of the new City Hall took place amid the ruins of the fire and brought many a real sign of hope. It was Prairie practicality at its best, a utilitarian structure that fit the needs of the moment and permitted urban life to continue.

Located on the southeast corner of LaSalle and Adams Streets, the building became known as "the Rookery." Though some said its name came about because of its rapid construction and dilapidated appearance, there had been a previous building on the site which was known for all the birds which nested nearby. The two-story brick building was built at a cost of $75,000 and was constructed around a massive, elevated water tank which serviced the southern section of the City before the fire. Most of the City's government offices were relocated to this building, and the first public library, subsequently, was located inside the water tank. Chicago actually never had a "public library" at this point. When Queen Victoria of England learned that Chicago had been destroyed and was told, incorrectly, that all the City's library books had burned, she and other British authors sent autograhed copies of their works to Chicago for a "new" library. When the books arrived there was no place to store them, so they were placed within the empty steel-drum water tank within the City Hall. Chicago's public library system thus had its humble birth.

The Common Council responded to Queen Victoria's generosity by sending a resolution of thanks to all English contributors in January of 1872.

Resolved. That the citizens of Chicago tender their thanks to Mr. Thomas Hughs, M.P., and those who have been his associates in England in undertaking to secure contributions of books for a Free Public Library in this City. We gratefully appreciate their labors on behalf of this most important object, and will use our utmost efforts to carry on and complete the great works so successfully commenced. (Common Council Resolution January 13, 1872)

Although this new City Hall building was never meant to be a permanent home for municipal government, the Rookery Building served as the Chicago City Hall for twelve years. Ironically as recovery was underway, a fire ordinance in the Common Council sparked a huge outcry among Chicago citizens who considered the government too weak. So worked up were they that on the evening of January 15, 1872 more than 10,000 marchers paraded through the City demanding a change in the ordinance. While walking through the fire-ravaged City on fresh snow, the demonstration soon turned violent when bricks were thrown through the windows of the new City Hall. Two bricks landed in the mayor's office. Many rioters were arrested when they took control of City Hall.

It will be long before Chicago hears the last of this disgraceful affair,—how her authorized legislative body was invaded by a howling mob, bearing threatening banners, its deliberations broken up, and its windows smashed, all by way of compelling the Council to vote as the rioters desired on a certain pending measure.

In spite of the fact that the police force on duty at the Council Chamber numbered eight men, the head of the procession was so powerful that they took immediate possession of the City Hall. (*Chicago Tribune*, January 17, 1872)

Mayor Joseph Medill (1871-1873) was arguably one of the most influential political figures to serve in the fifth City Hall. He developed several programs as mayor to mold the City's post-fire environment and was an important leader in the rapid rebuilding of the City after the Great Fire. Carter Harrison I (1879-1887, 1893) was elected as Mayor in 1879 and is noted for his work with the World's Columbian Exposition and the 1880 and 1884 Republican National Conventions.

The endeavor to refashion Chicago into a vibrant American city was perhaps one of the greatest undertakings in the history of urban America. From the financial investments of eastern bankers to the architects whose dreams would return life to the City, it was a breathtaking moment in the nation's history. No one said it better than Chicago's 28th Mayor—*We have rebuilt in five years a marvelous city out of the ashes and broken fortunes of the old: for years we have been carrying on the most gigantic system of public improvements, and have rivaled in a short time the works of our oldest cities.* (Inaugural Address, Mayor Monroe Heath, July 24, 1876)

MEDILL.

Sixth City Hall
1885-1908

"All architecture is shelter, all great architecture is the design of space that contains, cuddles, exalts, or stimulates the persons in that space."
Philip Johnson

On November 29, 1885, the *Chicago Tribune* reported on the details and interior beauty of the new City Hall, the City's sixth—*The most elaborate work is in the main vestibule, which has been done in the Louis XIV style. On the walls are emblematic panels suggestive of the arts, sciences, navigation, etc., and the ceiling is adorn with the seals of the State, country, city, and Union, with ornamentation to correspond to the Renaissance period.*

The French-Renaissance sixth City Hall. Photograph courtesy of the Chicago History Museum.

Council Chamber seen from the seating area at the back of the room. April 9, 1903. DN-0000398, *Chicago Daily News* negatives collection, Chicago History Museum.

The people of Chicago had never seen anything like it. City government had wrapped itself in the ethos of the Renaissance—a style most ordinary Chicagoans had never been introduced to before. Finally after the long night of the Great Fire's shadow, there was a municipal building of which every Chicagoan could be proud. But its fabrication was anything but simple. And despite the externals of beauty and taste, too much bickering; too many short-cuts and corner-cuts would doom the finished product to a short life—less than 20 years.

The story of Chicago's sixth City Hall is a protracted project of some dozen years. Soon after the Great Fire of 1871, both the City and County agreed to construct a building on the same location where the previous Courthouse/City Hall structure once stood. Both governments recognized the necessity of fashioning a permanent structure they could both occupy once more, and considered the Rookery Building on LaSalle and Adams Streets to be a temporary solution.

Less than four years following the Great Fire, the political disharmony and unabashed questionable maneuvers of local political leaders imperiled any successful rebuilding of a joint County/City government complex. Before a shovel of earth was moved great controversy would surround the projected development of a joint venture. Though the agencies sponsored a "competition," it was anything but smooth, resulting in wholesale larceny on the part of many—including the man who eventually would design and build the project, James J. Egan.

Since the city began to rise from its ashes the matter of a building of a new Court-House has served as a bone of contention in the County Board and City Council. When all other questions waned and lost interest in either of these bodies, a resolution looking to the beautifying of the old Court-House Square was sure to stir up the greatest interest, to excite the deepest attention, and draw forth the slumbering oratory of the leaders of the several "rings" which, for the last few years, have held almost unlimited control of both bodies. (*Chicago Tribune*, August 27, 1875)

The Board of Public Works, financed by funds left over from the reconstruction of the City's burned bridges, collaborated with the Cook County Board of Supervisors in the development of a design for new structure. In June of 1872, the City and County announced an architectural competition in order to select the best design for the new building.

Although Otto H. Matz was announced as the winner of the competition, neither the City of Chicago nor Cook County had much interest in building his winning design.

The County then moved to give the commission for the new complex to the third place architect, Thomas Tilly who had furnished a general plan for the buildings, City and County, in the shape of a Greek cross. His work was, at first, highly prized. Then, suddenly, Tilly could do nothing right. There soon followed a series of bitter encounters and public denouncements by members of the Cook County Board and the Common Council. Tilly refused to make the necessary design modifications they insisted upon and later withdrew. He was ham-strung by the politicians who appeared to have little personal regard for him or the constituencies they represented. The arguments continued for months throughout 1875. Many believe that the controversies were manufactured by political insiders within the County government in an attempt to make life so difficult for Tilly that he would be forced to withdraw from the project.

A similar scenario accounted for the sudden and mysterious rise in popularity of architect James J. Egan, an Irishman who made his reputation designing churches. He appears to have been a political insider with local officials who appeared very "eager" to have him on board for the project. Ironically, Egan received no recognition in the architectural competition for the complex. His design which was accepted had not been submitted to the contest committee. Egan was flexible and responsive to the suggestions of local politicians. He easily reached an agreement with the County and was given full control of the building project. The City government, wishing to save money, considered simply redrawing the County's plans for a mirror image for its building, but with further consideration it enlisted the services of architect John Mills Van Osdel to copy only the exterior design. Van Osdel had been the designer of the fourth City Hall.

The initial groundbreaking for the County Building took place on August 26, 1875, at the very zenith of the controversies surrounding the architects. Construction began after a short ceremony but it would not be completed until 1882, seven years after ground was broken. The building was to be a six-story, brick and stone French Renaissance structure with monumental 35-foot granite Corinthian columns. With funding secure, the County began construction first. After many delays and a prolonged construction period, the County Building was completed in 1882, with the completion of City Hall three years later in late 1884/1885. The combined construction costs for the City and the County totaled over $4 million.

Granger Harms was a political insider and the contractor who received the commission from the Cook County Board to fabricate the County Building's foundation. The *Chicago Tribune* was quick to point out that this was precisely the area where the most damage could be done to the project with opportunities to "swindle" the public by incompetence and improper work. *It is a matter of great importance that the foundation should be solidly laid, and it behooves the tax-payers to keep their eyes open, or they will be cheated from the start.* (*Chicago Tribune,* November 6, 1875)

By December 1, 1875, the *Chicago Tribune* was reporting egregious examples of the use of faulty materials for the foundation and questioning the ethics of Mr. Harms. *A Tribune reporter entered Building Superintendent Bailey's office in the City Hall, and took a glance over the complaint-book which lies open to all, and shows that Harms is driving rotten and condemned swamp-elm piles; and the question is, How long will this thing last? Inspector Agnew is on the ground all day, and since last week has condemned eight piles.*

When questions arose about the use of faulty materials and a reporter approached Cook County Commissioner Thomas Lonergan, he was quick with his response—*It's nobody's business; the Commissioners know what they were about.* (*Chicago Tribune,* December 1, 1875)

Once completed, the shortcomings of the building quickly became evident. The interior featured high ceilings, small windows, oddly sized rooms and long, dark corridors which ultimately proved ill-suited for the day-to-day business of City government. Furthermore, due to the lengthy construction process, the building reached maximum capacity prior to its completion, forcing many municipal employees to be moved into nearby rented space. Due to the inconvenience and discomfort, the two governments immediately began planning the construction of an even larger building which could be both architecturally significant as well as functional. Proposals from a number of sources were examined, several of which included plans for yet another dominating and grand structure. These plans were rejected, as many critics thought the existing City Hall already symbolized all that was wrong with the government, declaring it was too big, too extravagant and too isolated from the people and the life of the City.

No one was more outspoken with his criticism of the new City Hall than Public Works Commissioner (and later Chicago's 31st mayor) DeWitt Creiger. He said—*It was poorly adapted to the purposes required and intended, the rooms not being the proper size to suit the necessities of several departments, and that a proper City-Hall should be erected on the "rookery" lot.* (*Chicago Tribune,* November 18, 1884)

The Council met in their new City Hall home for the first time on the evening of November 17, 1884. One hundred Chicago citizens were invited to attend the opening of the Chamber located on the fourth floor on the LaSalle Street side. The room was sixty-feet wide, including the gallery, and ninety-two feet long. The *Chicago Tribune* was effusive in its description of the new Common Council Chamber.

The walls and the wainscoting are of white ash and the ceiling is gorgeous with blue paint and gold. Light is furnished by six large chandeliers, with sixty jets. The floor is covered with a Brussels carpet, and

The Sixth City Hall's entrance on LaSalle Street with a horse drawn carriage along the sidewalk in the foreground. 1906. DN-0050649, *Chicago Daily News* negatives collection, Chicago History Museum.

Mayor Fred A. Busse sitting behind his desk in the temporary City Hall at the Lehmann Building at 200 W. Randolph Street during construction of New City Hall. 1910. DN-0056245, *Chicago Daily News* negatives collection, Chicago History Museum.

Office in City Hall with
two policemen sitting on
duty. 1906. DN-0003825,
Chicago Daily News
negatives collection,
Chicago History Museum.

Temporary City Council
Chamber in the Lehmann
Building looking towards
the speaker's rostrum during
the construction of New
City Hall. 1908. DN-0006772,
Chicago Daily News
negatives collection,
Chicago History Museum.

Empty City Council Chamber of Sixth City Hall with podium. April 9, 1903. DN-0000397, *Chicago Daily News* negatives collection, Chicago History Museum.

Sixth City Hall building with rubble from the demolition of the adjacent County Building in the foreground. 1906. DN-0003849, *Chicago Daily News* negatives collection, Chicago History Museum.

all furniture is solid mahogany. The mayor's desk is in the center, the City Clerk's directly in front, and those of the Aldermen are arranged in semi-circular form. At the south end is a wardrobe, and north are two ante-rooms, which may be used by the committees, as no others are available. There are accommodations for about fifty spectators on the floor, in the corners, and about 400 more in the gallery. The new quarters are very pretty and comfortable, and the Aldermen are pleased. (*Chicago Tribune,* November 18, 1884)

Commissioner DeWitt Cregier presented Mayor Carter Harrison, I, with a special gavel to commemorate the first Common Council meeting in the new Chamber, fashioned from timber from old Fort Dearborn.

The City Hall had been constructed at a cost of almost one million dollars less than the cost of constructing the County Building to which it was connected. The County Building cost $2,424,668, while the City Hall cost $1,642,638 despite the fact that both buildings had the same dimensions. The difference came to $782,630, plus another $125,000 in special adjustments for a total of $907,603 in cost differentiations.

Though the Common Council met in November 1884, it would be three full months before Chicago's other municipal offices fully moved in to their new space. By January 23, 1885 the Water Department, Building Department and offices of the Department of Public Works (except the Commissioner) had made their way from the Rookery Building. By the next day the Offices of the City Treasurer were in their new home, together with all remaining City departments. By January 25, 1885 the Rookery was emptied.

Mayor Carter Harrison, I, made a visit to his new office on January 12, 1885 and surveyed the surroundings and found them ready for occupancy. But he decided to wait until, as he said, *the carpenters are through with the noisy part of their work.* (*Chicago Tribune,* January 13, 1885)

The Health Department, the Chicago Police Department and the Chicago Fire Department were all housed in the basement of City Hall. The Health Department took up the entire southwest corner and

the Police Department filled the entire east side of the lower level. The office of the Chief of Police was housed just inside the south entrance of the Building on LaSalle Street; the Fire Alarm and Telegraph Office just south and the Fire Department just north of the north entrance on LaSalle Street. South of the main entrance was the Office of the Mayor; nearby was the Comptroller's Office on the west side, filling the southwest corner. On the east side was the Office of the City Treasurer and the City Clerk's Office.

On the second floor were the offices of the Department of Public Works. The City Engineer had his office in the southwest corner. In the northwest corner was the Department of Sewers. The Law Department had its office on the third floor, the northwest half of the floor, while the Board of Education occupied the southern half of the floor above the main entrance on LaSalle Street.

The *Chicago Tribune* gave visitors some advice for making their way around the new building—*The third floor is best reached by way of the County Building, with which it is connected by a well-sheltered passageway over the rotunda. It would indeed be a good plan, pondering the construction of the elevators for the City Hall, to have the connection between City Hall and County Building cleared on all floors.* (*Chicago Tribune,* January 23, 1885)

Chicago's climate and the everyday wear and tear on the building soon became apparent. Despite an energetic program of maintenance and repair, the building on each side began to disintegrate more rapidly than anyone could have projected. It was readily apparent to everyone who used the buildings that something was not right.

Because there was no money for either government to construct a new building so soon, the plans for newer structures were entirely theoretical. Despite the building's shortcomings, both the City and County occupied the structure for over two decades. It was not until the January of 1905, when an explosion damaged the County side of the building, that talk of construction became increasingly realistic. The foundation of the building had begun to deteriorate.

The Drake Fountain at the LaSalle Street entrance of City Hall in 1906. It was a gift from Chicago hotelier John B. Drake (inset). This granite water fountain, designed by architect Richard Henry Park, was placed there in 1892 to mark the 400th anniversary of the voyage of Christopher Columbus. The fountain provided chilled water from four granite basins. A statue of Christopher Columbus stands at the front of the fountain. In 1909 it was moved to the far southside, to 92nd Street at South Chicago and Exchange Avenues. It remains a Chicago landmark. 1908. DN-0053397, *Chicago Daily News* negatives collection, Chicago History Museum.

Old City Hall being demolished with the building's exterior walls partially intact and cranes inside the shell. 1908. DN-0053356, *Chicago Daily News* negatives collection, Chicago History Museum.

LaSalle Street traffic running past Chicago's Sixth City Hall. 1890s, Chicago History Museum, *Chicago Daily News* Photo Archive DN 0006234.

Building debris from the demolition of the old City Hall, seen from across LaSalle street at ground level. 1908. DN-0053505, *Chicago Daily News* negatives collection, Chicago History Museum.

Sixth City Hall Building seen from LaSalle and Washington streets after the demolition of the formerly adjacent County Building. 1906. DN-0003850, *Chicago Daily News* negatives collection, Chicago History Museum.

Two views of the Old Sixth City Hall at far left adjacent to the County Building nearly complete, with a streetcar in front of the County Building. 1910. DN-000161, DN-061625, *Chicago Daily News* negatives collection, Chicago History Museum.

Wrecking of the old City Hall building. 1908. DN-0006725, *Chicago Daily News* negatives collection, Chicago History Museum.

Mayor Carter Harrison, courtesy of Chicago History Museum photo archive.

Demolition of old Sixth City Hall with new County Building behind, 1908. DN-0053356, *Chicago Daily News* negatives collection, Chicago History Museum.

Aldermen Mike Sullivan, John E. Scully, Michael Kenna, Patrick White, and John Matalin. DN-0052814, *Chicago Daily News* negatives collection, Chicago History Museum.

Paying taxes, men and women forming a line extending down a hallway and through a door in the City Hall building. 1905. DN-0003075, *Chicago Daily News* negatives collection, Chicago History Museum.

The explosion and ensuing fire left one dead and five injured. Frightening deficiencies in the building's safety provisions and the failure to comply with ordinances requiring adequate fire escapes, of which the building was almost completely devoid, provoked serious reconsideration of the integrity of the structure. Just over one year earlier, the absence of similar fire safety measures had caused the deaths of over 600 people in the Iroquois Theater, resulting in the deadliest fire in Chicago history. Although that tragedy had sparked a sweeping reform of City safety ordinances, the City Hall building had not yet conformed to the new requirements. Fire safety was an overriding priority in reaching the decision to abandon the County/City Hall complex and construct a new building for the City and County. Once again combining their resources, they began negotiating a solution to their dilemma.

Despite the turmoil regarding the sixth City Hall, it witnessed many historical events of civic importance. Chicago's population had reached an unprecedented 1,698,000 by the turn of the century, with one out of every 10,000 residents owning an automobile. Mayor Carter Henry Harrison, I, served as mayor from 1879 to 1887, and again in 1893, describing the City he loved as "his bride." During the night of the Haymarket Riot in 1886, Harrison had been able to navigate through a volatile crowd of protesters, labor activists and anarchists. The protest was organized in response to an initiative on behalf of the 8-hour work day. During the protest, an unknown person threw a bomb which knocked down 60 policemen, killing one and fatally wounding seven others, provoking police to open fire into the crowd.

Harrison went on to oversee the construction of the first elevated, "El," railway in the downtown area in 1891 as well as the 1893 opening of the World's Columbian Exposition, which attracted nearly 29 million visitors throughout the six month event. Many successful inventions and products were first introduced at the World's Fair, including Cracker Jacks, the Vienna Kosher Hot Dog, Juicy Fruit Gum, Pabst Blue Ribbon Beer and a 250-foot high attraction built by George Ferris. At the Fair many Americans viewed their first telephone; their first electric light bulb; their first voice recording device; and their first moving picture machine. The imagination of the world was dazzled and amazed.

The night before the Exposition came to a close, a mentally ill disgruntled, office seeker, named Richard Prendergast, went to Harrison's home at Ashland Avenue and Jackson Boulevard and, when admitted, shot and killed the beloved patrician mayor. Closing ceremonies of the Fair the following day became a somber memorial to Chicago's genteel, aristocratic mayor. From around the world people visited the Exposition celebrating Columbus' four hundredth anniversary of his arrival in the New World. Its success came in achieving Harrison's great goal of showing the world the "true Chicago," a city which was alive with the spirit of the modern world. It was the fastest growing city on the planet earth and was bigger and better than it had been just two decades earlier when the Great Fire ravaged it. Its rapid growth would continue. In the distance a seventh City Hall building was ready to rise once more, beyond the scope and shape anyone had anticipated.

Two aldermen standing in the City Hall section of the Illinois Tunnel system below the building on LaSalle Street. 1907. DN-0005301, *Chicago Daily News* negatives collection, Chicago History Museum.

Alderman and Carnival Manager John E. Scully wrestling with a bear at the Madison Street Carnival. August 14, 1904. DN-0001220, *Chicago Daily News* negatives collection, Chicago History Museum.

Alderman Joseph Badenoch, reading a newspaper in City Hall. 1911. DN-0009146, *Chicago Daily News* negatives collection, Chicago History Museum.

Mayor Edward Fitzsimmons Dunne sitting at the speaker's desk in the Council Chamber of the Sixth City Hall. 1905. DN-0003628, *Chicago Daily News* negatives collection, Chicago History Museum.

Aldermen hear testimony in the Council Chamber during the Iroquois Theater investigation. January 1904. DN-0001800, *Chicago Daily News* negatives collection, Chicago History Museum.

The Current and
Seventh City Hall
1909-Present

"Maybe we can show government how to operate better as a result of better architecture. Eventually, I think Chicago will be the most beautiful great city left in the world."
Frank Lloyd Wright

On January 16, 1905, twenty-years after the construction of the Sixth City Hall, a disaster struck the County Building/City Hall complex of wide proportions. A radical settling of the south end of the County Building by more than six inches in a 24-hour period caused a rupture in some gas pipes located on the fourth floor of the County portion of the complex. Building workers were searching for the gas leak when a careless spark caused a massive explosion that took the life of Thomas Edwards, the County's Chief Painter. He succumbed to severe burns to his body and face. Five other people were injured—a fireman, two painters, a deputy sheriff, and a bailiff in the County Courthouse.

One painter jumped through a window and crawled along the building's ledge to the courtroom of Judge Edward Fitzsimmons Dunne (later Chicago's 38th Mayor and Illinois' 24th Governor.) Damage to the County Building was so severe that the Washington Street entranced had to be closed.

In addition, it was discovered that the complex was in serious violation of existing City codes. The lack of any fire escapes in the 1885 complex and the peril presented to employees by their absence was yet a further factor in cause for alarm. It was also feared that any further disaster would seriously imperil important documents of the courts, and records of the Board of Assessors Office and other governmental agencies. This led to a close inspection of the entire complex. It was discovered that as much as three to ten tons of stone were ready to collapse on the Clark Street pavement from the uppermost reaches of the building. A report in the *Chicago Tribune* indicated that damage by the explosion and fire were the least of the structural problems faced by the building's joint complex. The fire caused less than $10,000 worth of damage, but the incident revealed further concerns. Strong support grew to raise the structure and begin again to fashion a more efficient, economical and structurally sound County/City Hall complex. Some critics, especially westside aldermen, supported the notion that a new governmental complex actually belonged further west from the downtown area so as to relieve the growing congestion along the central City thoroughfares.

Officials of the County were of one voice in urging the construction of a new facility. *The present structure is sagging and is dangerous*, Cook County Commissioner Christopher Strassheim told the *Chicago Tribune*. E. H. Olsen, Chairman of the Building Committee said—*The present structure was built twenty-five years ago at a time when people were too much impressed with the desirability of patronizing home industries to satisfy themselves whether the material would stand the damp climate of Chicago. The increase in population was not taken into consideration.* (The *Chicago Tribune*, January 24, 1905)

Support for the construction of a new City/County complex had grown and intensified. The project of necessity was driven by the needs of the County. Cook County Board President Edward J. Brundage said—*It is believe this is a propitious time for the allegation of the subject of the new building. If prompt steps are taken it will be possible to submit the question to a vote of the people at the spring election. The County has no plans for the building except that it should be large enough and modern, especially with respect to light and ventilation.* (The *Chicago Tribune*, January 24, 1905)

Cook County Commissioner Julian Mack described what was thought to be the proper parameters for any new design—*The new building should extend to the lot line. The present structure is inadequate, dangerous and unsightly. I have talked with many persons, and all are in favor of a new courthouse. It is a source of danger to all who enter it or who use the adjoining streets.* (*Chicago Tribune*, January 24, 1905)

When the City of Chicago and Cook County decided that construction of a new structure was imperative, they eschewed potential new locations on the westside or on the lake front which were briefly considered before it was determined to remain in the same traditional location between Clark and LaSalle Streets and Washington and Randolph Streets. Once again as they had in June of 1872, the City and County jointly conducted an architectural competition to determine the design of the building.

The County invited the City to be a partner in the new joint venture. The plan called for the County to construct its building of a courthouse and center for County government first, and then move ahead with the City's efforts to construct its building. The imperative was more urgent on the part of the County since its building had sustained damage in the recent explosion and the general deteriorating condition of its structure. The two structures were to be erected conjointly. It was to be a "double structure," roughly costing some $6,000,000.

Chairman Edwin K. Walker of the Cook County Finance Committee said—*The site was dedicated for city and county purposes and the*

New City Hall building
during construction,
nearly complete. 1910.
DN-0008404, *Chicago Daily
News* negatives collection,
Chicago History Museum.

Architects William Holabird
(top) and Martin Roche

Burnham's Civic Center—the hub of all government enterprises, including a fresh new Civic Center set at Congress Parkway and Halsted Street—would have plunged the cityscape into a Parisian fantasy. Burnham's *Plan of Chicago 1909* was a fantastic urban architectural dream.

When City and County leaders chose to remain at the old location of the Courthouse Square for the project, Burnham lost interest in any design for a new City Hall-County building.

Balance, proportion, urban scale and tasteful design were
all part of Burnham's plan for a modern reshaping of the
of the Chicago Metropolis' prairie character, providing it with
a fresh geographical axis for its urban government. His plan,
invisioned here, never came to be.

Foundation caissons, new City Hall, 1909.
Chicago History Museum.

Foundation work at the
new City Hall. Looking down
caisson well–Depth 100.5 ft,
diameter 9.5 ft. 1909.
Chicago History Museum.

City Hall Cornerstone laying, Public Works Commissioner Bernard J. Mullaney addresses crowd from North LaSalle and Washington Streets. 1909. DN-0054873, *Chicago Daily News* negatives collection, Chicago History Museum.

To the far right of the frame is architect Louis Sullivan and Dankmar Adler's famed arch-entrance to the Chicago Stock Exchange Building.

Laying of the
Seventh City Hall Cornerstone,
Chicago City Hall Archive.

New City Hall and County
Building from West Washington
Street looking east. 1910.
DN-0008175, *Chicago Daily
News* negatives collection,
Chicago History Museum.

City Hall cornerstone laying ceremony. Alderman Francis Taylor standing next to the cornerstone. 1909. DN-0054872, *Chicago Daily News* negatives collection, Chicago History Museum.

Mr. Michael Faherty (2nd from right), President of the Board of Local Improvements and Mrs. Faherty, 1928. DN-0084410, *Chicago Daily News* negatives collection, Chicago History Museum.

structures cannot well be separated. My idea would be to erect a practical building that would at the same time have some individuality to distinguish it from surrounding structures. (*Chicago Tribune*, January 24, 1905)

By March 1905, two months following the County Building explosion, in the waning days of Mayor Carter Harrison II's administration, a joint committee with the County considered the needs and difficulties of constructing a new City Hall. The question of the financial ability of the City to build at that time and of the very necessity of the need for a new structure was left to this sub-committee. It was felt that any new structure would have to be uniform in design to that of the County Building.

The *City side is a much better structure than the county, and perhaps never will crumble as the latter will,* said City Building Commissioner Williams. *However, the rooms from a sanitary standpoint are not fit for people to work in. There is more money spent for repairs and alterations than a new building would cost in the long run.*

In June 1906, following a negative report on the City Hall by City Engineer, George W. Jackson, he recommended that the present "ruin" of City Hall be destroyed and a sub-committee was delegated to devise the ways and means for the construction of a new municipal building. He stated—*It would be more advisable to abandon and destroy the crumbling ruin than to attempt to repair and preserve it through an indefinite period of years. It would be cheaper for the city to rent space in other buildings than to maintain the present building. The cost of maintenance is $85,000 a year.* (*Chicago Tribune*, June 12, 1906)

Six months later, in January 1907, a very confident 7th Ward Alderman Frank I. Bennett, the Chairmen of the City Council Committee on Finance, suggested that the present structure should be torn down at once. *I expect the City Council will appropriate one million dollars for a new city hall when the annual budget is made up next month. I think the present building should be torn down at once, and work begun on a new and modern*

structure suitable to the needs. It is a waste of money to continue occupying the old unsanitary building. (*Chicago Tribune*, January 1, 1907)

Within two months, March 5, 1907, the Chicago City Council ordered a new City Hall to be constructed, but not without controversy. By a vote of 33 to 29 the Council passed the measure for their new home at the LaSalle and Randolph Street site. Thirty-three alderman from the north and southside pushed through the measure to join to the County Building structure. Twenty-nine westside aldermen attempted to move the City Hall to Union Park at the corner of Washington Boulevard and Ashland Avenue, two miles west of the downtown area. *It is the intention to make the building the duplicate in size and appearance of the nearly completed County Building which it will adjoin,* the *Chicago Tribune* reported.

Alderman Bennett explained that the money for the new building would come not from saloon revenue, as had been proposed, but from bond accounts. After the defeat of the westside proposition, the order passed by a *viva voce* vote. Earlier, ten architectural firms—six well-known Chicago-based companies and four out-of-town firms—presented designs for the shared City Hall/County Building project already underway by the time the City Council maneuvered legislation for a new City Hall component. Those presenting architectural plans were among the finest architects in America.

Holabird & Roche, produced the winning design, an eleven-story Grecian Temple with eleven exterior Corinthian columns on each of the long profiles of the structure along Clark Street on the east and LaSalle Street on the west; and eight similar columns each on the north face along Randolph Street and the south face on Washington Street. The design filled the entire footprint of the full city block square. The Holabird & Roche design received twelve positive votes out of the fifteen-member board, counting the president. Two Commissioners, Umbach and Garner, cast their ballots for the design Barnett, Haynes & Barnett of St. Louis.

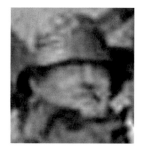

Alderman Frank I. Bennett, 7th Ward (1901-1909) Finance Chair (1905-1909), former Commissioner of Public Works. DN-0069958, *Chicago Daily News* negatives collection, Chicago History Museum.

The massive acanthus leaves on the capital of a corinthian column of the new City Hall building. 1910. DN-0008852, *Chicago Daily News* negatives collection, Chicago History Museum.

A sculpture at the entrance of new City Hall is installed DN-0005726, *Chicago Daily News* negatives collection, Chicago History Museum.

Building expert Talbot and architect Wells inspecting City Hall. 1911. DN-0008918, *Chicago Daily News* negatives collection, Chicago History Museum.

Building directory in the entrance hall of the new County Building. 1908. DN-0006690, *Chicago Daily News* negatives collection, Chicago History Museum.

Electrical control center
at new City Hall, 1926.
DN-0080203, *Chicago Daily
News* negatives collection,
Chicago History Museum.

Murals inside the Council
Chamber by artist Frederick
Clay Bartlett, depicting
significant Chicago industries.
1911. DN-0009480B,
Chicago Daily News negatives
collection, Chicago History
Museum.

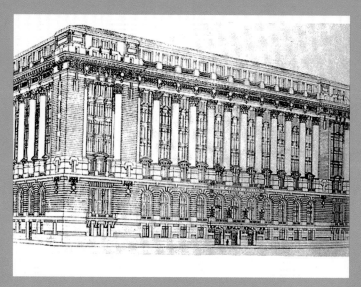

Chicago City Hall/County Building competition, Shepley, Rutan and Coolidge perspective. From *Western Architect*, September 1905.

Chicago City Hall/County Building competition, Barnett, Haynes and Barnett perspective. From *Western Architect*, September 1905.

Chicago City Hall/County Building competition, Holabird & Roche perspective. From *Western Architect*, September 1905.

Holabird & Roche was a well-known and popular Chicago architectural partnership that had already captured the imagination of Chicagoans with a series of architectural triumphs. It was a "legacy" firm of refined designers. They knew Chicago and understood Chicagoans. The firm had a feel for local politics and what the essentials were to be incorporated into the design. While their plans were elegant and classical, they also incorporated a critical understanding of the multi-use purposes of a structure required to serve the needs of both City and County governments.

Holabird & Roche had already designed some treasured pieces of Chicago architecture, efficient workplaces where commerce was conducted, businesses operated and industry flourished. Highly functional and intelligent, their buildings brightened the local landscape by their sense of modern and effective engineering. Among their more well-known works are their addition to the Monadnock Building (1891), the Marquette Building (1895), the Old Colony Building (1894), the Three Arts Club (1914), and Soldier Field (1924), as well as the Chicago Board of Trade (1930) under the name of Holabird & Root as the firm came to be known. The "Chicago window"—one large pane with two side sash panes—became one of their singular design elements. In Chicago there is high appreciation for great design and architecture. It is, after all, the "coin of the realm" here. If Holabird & Roche had a modern eye and a smooth hand for grand design some of the credit must go to their remarkable mentor William LeBaron Jenney. It was while working in Jenney's Chicago architectural studio that William Holabird and Martin Roche first met. Jenney, thought by many to be "the father of the American skyscraper," had a deep influence on the young pair of architects. His ten-story Home Insurance Building (1885) on LaSalle Street is still considered the first American skyscraper. Jenney gave Chicago its first architectural triumph and set it on the road to becoming the nation's most important capital of architecture.

County Board President Brundage summed it all up when he said—*Everything considered, the plans of Holabird and Roche comes nearest to meeting the requirements of the county, especially the interior arrangement. Plenty of light has been provided for, and that is regarded as an extremely important feature.* (*Chicago Tribune,* January 24, 1905)

A problem arose following the award when some members of the County Board suggested that Holabird & Roche had not won the competition fairly. They felt that Shepley, Rutan & Coolidge, the New York firm who had designed the Chicago Public Library (1892) on Michigan Avenue, should have been awarded joint supervision of the project because of their ideas regarding elevation of the design. President Brundage asked William Holabird how he felt about working in partnership with another architectural firm. Holabird did not mince words in his rejection of the idea.

Holabird responded—*I have been an architect here for thirty years, and have built many of the big modern buildings in the downtown district, and I don't fancy the idea of working with anybody else.* (*Chicago Tribune,* August 29, 1905)

Also submitting designs in competition for the project were:

● **D.H. Burnham and Company**—the firm established by the great Daniel H. Burnham, himself, and John Wellborn Root (1850-1891)—Chicago's most revered architects who fashioned many outstanding local buildings like the Reliance Building (1894-95), the mother of all glass and steel framed buildings; as well as the force behind the grand scale designs for the World's Columbian Exposition of 1893. Though Burnham submitted a design, the plans were later withdrawn. He was busy creating his famed 1909 Plan of Chicago with Edward H. Bennett. This plan envisioned a colossal urban setting for a governmental building design for the future. In his plan this structure was the axis of the city. All of Chicago was to be recalibrated and re-centered with a Civic Center of mammoth proportions located at Halsted Street and Congress Parkway.

This building's great dome from which all City streets radiated was deeply in the Parisian style, much like Baron Haussmann's re-design of the French capital between 1852-1870. Burnham had little interest in a civic center at the same old site of LaSalle and Randolph Streets as its predecessors. Although Burnham's design was not accepted, still today his vision of Chicago is the most lofty and, at times, inches its influence into contemporary urban design.

● **Frost and Granger,** the architects who gave the City the Coliseum (1900); the LaSalle Street Station (1903), the Northern Trust Bank (1905) and Navy Pier (1916) submitted their own design plan.

● **Huehl and Schmid** also threw their hat into the ring. They would be the creators of the 4,200 seat Moorish-style Medinah Temple (1910), today known as the Bloomingdale Home and Furniture Store.

● **Jarvis Hunt** likewise submitted designs. He was well known as the designer of the Pompeian Village at the Columbian Exposition (1892), the Vermont Building (1892), also at the World's Fair, as well as the famed 30 N. Michigan Avenue Building (1914), the Lake Shore Athletic Club (1924) and the Great Lakes Naval Training Station (1911) in the far northern suburbs.

● And of course, the man who gave the city its most important architectural aphorism— *"form follows function"*– the incomparable **Louis Sullivan,** also was involved in the competition. His most important impact on Chicago architecture was the Auditorium Building Complex of an Opera House, Hotel and Office Building. It was the City's tallest building when it opened in 1889. Adler & Sullivan had their office and studio in the building's tower. Sullivan and his studio apprentice, Frank Lloyd Wright, designed the Transportation Building (1892) for the Columbian Exposition. In addition Sullivan designed the famed Carson Pirie Scott Department Store on State Street (1899).

Also submitting designs were four non-Chicago architectural firms:

● **Shepley, Rutan and Coolidge** (the firm that inherited H.H. Richardson's Boston practice) had been a favorite of Chicagoans because of their elegant design for the City's Public Library on Michigan Avenue (1892) as well as the Art Institute of Chicago (1892).

● The New York Firm of **Carrere and Hastings,** well-known for their elaborate New York Public Library (1897-1911) and the Triumphal Bridge (1901) for the Pan American Games both demonstrating dramatic classical temperament, submitted a design.

● So too did the New York firm of **George B. Post & Sons,** the designers of the New York Stock Exchange (1903) in the style of a classical Greek Temple, the Beaux-Arts-influenced Wisconsin State Capital (1906) and the Manufacturers and Liberal Arts Building (1892) at the Columbian Exposition.

● The St. Louis firm of **Barnett, Haynes & Barnett, George I. Barnett, principal,** also submitted a design that was evocative of their long and well-respected career fashioning public buildings and churches. Barnett was known as one of America's most able classicists, a man who had little use for modern innovations.

The overwhelming majority of the joint committee was committed to its selection of Holabird & Roche. They signed a contract on December 11, 1905 to begin construction on the County side of the building. Drilling began just over one month later, on January 18, 1906, and the cornerstone was laid on March 21. County workers moved into their building on July 6, 1907.

While construction on the eastern half of the building progressed rapidly, the City did not begin construction of its portion of the building until April 15, 1909. The City was forced to delay as it waited for the State of Illinois to expand its revenue bonds

Half completed front wall on the new City Hall and Courthouse building. 1907. DN-0004898, *Chicago Daily News* negatives collection, Chicago History Museum.

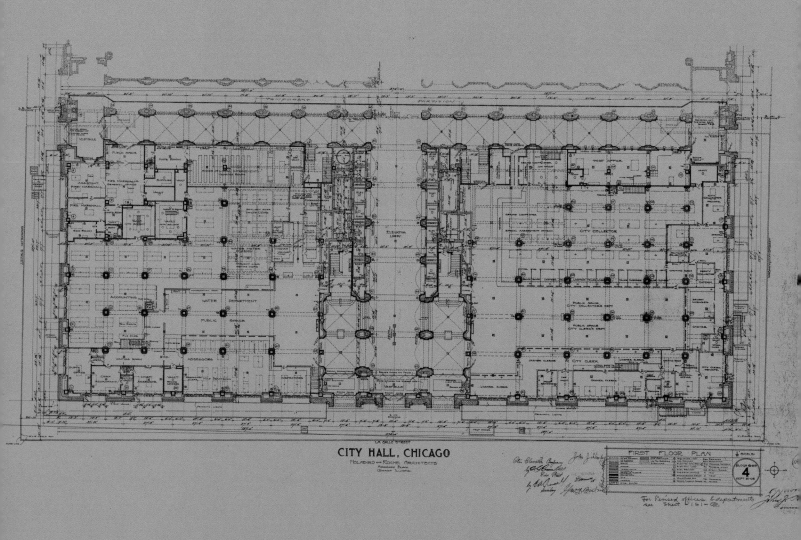

CITY HALL, CHICAGO

HOLABIRD AND ROCHE, ARCHITECTS

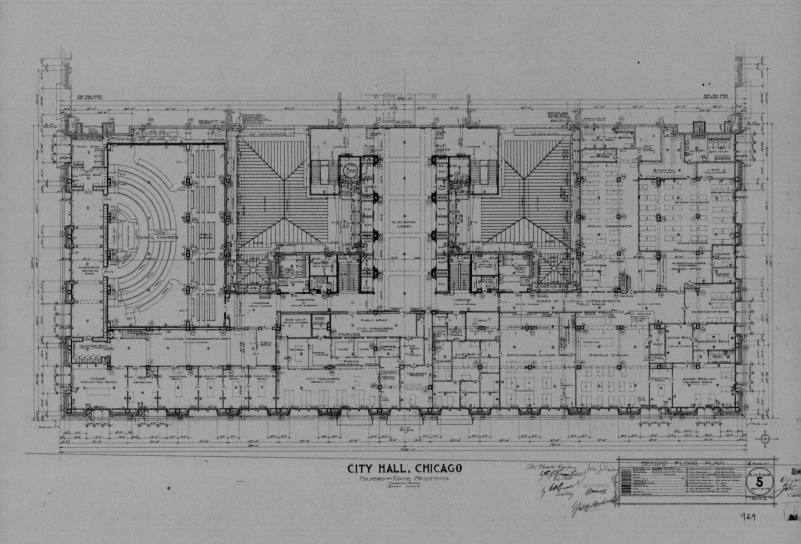

CITY HALL, CHICAGO

Holabird and Roche, Architects

Chicago City Council meets in the new Chambers. 1911. DN-0009028, *Chicago Daily News* negatives collection, Chicago History Museum.

Mayor "Big Bill" Thompson at his desk in City Hall, talking with railway employees about their living conditions. July 14, 1915. DN-0064829, *Chicago Daily News* negatives collection, Chicago History Museum.

in order to finance the structure. After the finances were arranged, City offices were moved to the new Courthouse so construction could take place.

The cornerstone of the new City Hall was laid on July 20, 1909 at a small ceremony largely devoid of any political or celebrity figures. A *Chicago Tribune* article called this "minimum of show...appropriate" and stressed the practicality and industry of the new building over its architectural décor (July 21, 1909). This stood in stark contrast to the laying of the County side cornerstone in 1906, which was attended by thousands of onlookers and the Vice President of the United States, Charles W. Fairbanks.

The present and seventh City Hall was completed and opened in February of 1911, with a very quiet ceremony; simple and restrained. Alderman Theodore Long delivered an address in the new City Council chamber and Mayor Fred Busse declined to sit in the ornate, new presiding chair. The reason for the lack of pomp and circumstance was the occasion of a Mayoral Primary the following day, which signaled the eventual election of Carter Henry Harrison II as Mayor, once again. While presiding over the Council from a smaller, more comfortable chair, Busse banged the gavel presented to him by Alderman Charles M. Foell, on behalf of the contractors who worked on the new structure, with such force at the opening of the session that he shattered it into pieces.

Alderman Long said in his oration—*If Chicago is to retain her proper place among the great constructive moral forces of this world, this beautiful temple must stand for more than the money expended in its construction and embellishment—more than the mere materialism which this money represents. It must stand for the highest ideal of citizenship, for the expanding spirit of Americanism, which means equal opportunity for all and special privileges for none, a square deal before the law, and a vigorous enforcement of its penalties against the public official who uses his office as a special privilege for the enrichment of himself or his client.* (*Chicago Tribune,* February 28, 1911)

As both buildings used the design plans of Holabird & Roche, the exterior of the massive granite edifice presented a unified, cohesive look to the outside world. The Cook County side of the building was completed before City Hall was built, but architects from Holabird & Roche took the chance that the new City Hall, when it materialized, would connect to the County Building and be of a twin design. Thus, the granite corners on the westside of the County Building were constructed in order that they could be removed and placed on City Hall instead of cutting new, expensive granite corners.

The inspiration for the design was monumental classicism, done in the Classical-Revival style. This had been a popular American architectural style in the late 19th and early 20th centuries, often used in churches and public buildings. It was noted for its symmetrical facades and minimal use of bays, towers or projecting elements. The building was fashioned in the ornate Corinthian order, with its most striking feature being the 87-foot-tall columns and Corinthian capitals. An entablature above the columns is 24-feet high and contains wreaths above each column. None of the hollow columns are fully freestanding from the building, but are disengaged enough so that they can employ entasis (the appearence that they are wider in the middle) to appear straight.

Four sculpted granite panels flank the entrance doors on LaSalle Street, representing four central aspects of City government. They depict Playgrounds, Schools, the Water System and the Park System. The Noel Construction Company was contracted to do the work, with John Flanagan making the original models and F.A. Purdy supervising the actual carving.

The graceful interior lobby features polished Botticino marble that soars over visitors in groined arches. Marble mosaics frame the arches, creating a look that is minimalistic, yet beautiful. The upper floors of the building were designed to be spacious and simple, allowing various departments to modify their offices according to individual needs.

Chicago City Council Chamber in City Hall during a council meeting. 1925. DN-0078452, *Chicago Daily News* negatives collection, Chicago History Museum.

Alderman Michael "Hinky Dink" Kenna of the 1st Ward from 1897-1923.

Window flower box at
City Hall, part of the plan
for the beautification
of buildings in Chicago.
July 27, 1914. DN-0063295,
Chicago Daily News
negatives collection,
Chicago History Museum.

The jewel of Chicago's City Hall has always been the two-story Council Chamber which sits on the westside of the building.

The original Council Chamber, measuring 65 feet by 96 feet, was ornately decorated in the Italian Renaissance style. The walls were oak-paneled and adorned with seven murals painted by the prestigious Chicago-born American painter Frederick Clay Bartlett (1873-1953). They were added in an attempt to display the "active, democratic spirit and the ability for accomplishing things, which seems to be typical of Chicago" (*Annual Report*, Department of Public Works, 1912). These murals represented:

● Electricity (placed over the Mayor's seat)
● The Building up of Chicago
● Labor
● Education
● The Gifts of Illinois to the Nation
● The Great Chicago Fire
● Commerce

On April 10, 1911, just two months after the opening of the new City Hall, a fire broke out. The blaze occurred in a vault in the southeast corner of the building's vault floor late in the afternoon. A janitress, Mrs. Mary Schultz, alerted people after smelling smoke as she went to clean in the area near the vault. Several thousand copies of City permits, stored in the vault, were the source of the fire. Chicago Police Officer Fred Kouka and Chicago Firefighter George O'Connor were quickly at the scene. The fire was beginning to make some real headway as they arrived. They were able to wheel a large chemical extinguisher to the fire and open it up on the flames. In the process they were almost overcome by the smoke and fumes caused by the dense smoke as the chemical wet the paper.

Kouka and O'Connor then raised an alarm and Engine Company No. 40 and Truck Company No. 6 responded at once and fought the blaze in relays of two for over an hour. Public Works Commissioner B.J. Mullaney raced to the scene and opened up a ventilation fan sending smoke out the elevator shafts. Little damage was done to the new building though the contents of the vault were destroyed.

Forty years later, on March 21, 1957, a more damaging fire began in the Chicago City Council Chambers and raged for two hours, destroying the Chambers, aldermanic offices on the second floor and other offices in the northwest corner of the building. Faulty wiring was thought to have started the conflagration, though others speculated that a careless cigar tossed by an alderman into a waste basket, may have been the real source. Investigators did determined that the extensive wood paneling, very heavily varnished, most likely added to the rapid spread of the flames. The City Council authorized $500,000 to repair the damage to the Chambers and other parts of City Hall.

Paul Gerhardt, a Chicago architect, was called upon to design the remodeling project. He eliminated the wood paneling and brought a modernistic look to the Chambers by using a mix of plaster, fireproof wood and stone. Seating capacity was increased by over 50 percent with the addition of a glass-enclosed balcony over the gallery. The new Chamber was dedicated on March 4, 1958, the 121st anniversary of the incorporation of the City of Chicago.

At the 40-minute dedication ceremony Mayor Richard J. Daley spoke, stating that *the [tale] of Chicago is a great American story.* He went on to state that Chicago is *a small Midwestern town that has grown into a great center of commerce and industry as well as a city of culture, religion, and education.* Daley reasoned that Chicago has great challenges that lie ahead in becoming the greatest metropolis in the world.

After the ceremony a luncheon was held at the Hotel Sherman, across the street from City Hall, where the praises continued. Among the guests were former Illinois Governor Adlai Stevenson, the Democratic Party's presidential nominee in 1952 and then again in 1956. Many of the City's Aldermen, including P. J. "Parky" Cullerton were present. He described the new Chambers as *modern and a symbol of the future.* The Associated Retail Bakers of Chicago presented the City with a 121st birthday present—an eight-foot tall, 600-pound birthday cake that sat on display in the lobby of City Hall.

Both the old and the new Council Chambers were the legislative home to many influential political personalities and decisive moments in Chicago's political history. Mayor William Hale "Big Bill" Thompson who served from 1915-1923 and again from 1927-1931, the last Republican Mayor of Chicago, once brought a rodeo into the City Council Chamber on February 2, 1931, horses included. Thompson was notorious for his ties to organized crime—including Al Capone, who backed his reelection campaign in 1927. Thompson was also noted for holding a debate between himself and two live rats, used to represent his opponents. While courting the Irish vote during his 1927 campaign, he threatened to punch the King of England, George V, in the nose, if he ever came to Chicago. His term witnessed both the Chicago race riots of 1919 and the St. Valentine's Day Massacre in 1929.

Former Cook County Board President Anton Cermak rode into office on a wave of public resentment after Thompson's controversial last term. Considered the father of the Chicago Political Machine, Cermak was assassinated by an Italian, characterized by the press as an anarchist, Giuseppe Zangara, during a 1933 fence-mending meeting in Miami Beach with President-elect Franklin Delano Roosevelt. Zangara was thought by many to be an assassin for the Nitti/Capone mob and was acting on their orders to shoot Cermak in retaliation for an attempt on the life of mob boss Frank Nitti in Chicago by Cermak's Chicago Police security detail. Cermak, not Roosevelt, was the intended target of Zangara's bullet. Cermak, a Czech immigrant, was forceful, persuasive and an effective politician—he, by and large, ended the Republican Party's power in Chicago.

More recent political figures have also called City Hall their home. Richard J. Daley (1955-1976) was Chicago's longest serving mayor (a record soon to be eclipsed by his son, Mayor Richard M. Daley) and its most widely-known, as well as Jane Byrne (1979-1983), Chicago's first female mayor; Harold Washington (1983-1987), the City's

first African-American mayor; Eugene Sawyer (1987-1988), the City's second African-American mayor; and Richard M. Daley (1989-Present), the City's current mayor.

Mayor Richard M. Daley has spearheaded efforts to continue the architectural and cultural significance of the City Hall building. In 2000, through the Urban Heat Island Initiative, a rooftop garden was envisioned as a means to test the benefits of green roofs and how they affect temperature and air quality. Interestingly, the idea for a rooftop garden had originated when the building first opened in 1911, but was not acted upon for nearly 100 years. A 20,300 square foot garden was completed in 2001, populated with 150 varieties of shrubs, vines, plants and trees, as well as a bee apiary producing a special brand of City Hall honey. The garden absorbs less heat from the sun than the previous tar roof and keeps City Hall cooler in the summer, requiring less energy for air conditioning.

With several small weather stations located on the City and County sides of the roof to monitor and compare air temperature, effects of the green roof on the larger neighborhood can be measured. Information gathered on a 90 degree afternoon in August 2001 at 1:45 p.m. determined the air temperature on the City Hall roof ranged between 126 and 130 degrees on the paved area and between 91 and 119 degrees on the planted space, both well under the 169 degree temperature measured on the black tar County roof. The lower temperature has led to direct energy savings during hot Chicago summers. If rooftop gardens were to be planted on a larger portion of the downtown buildings, green roof advocates say it would be reasonable to expect lower air temperatures and higher air quality throughout the city. Additionally, the garden improves air quality, reduces storm water runoff and lessens the effects of urban heat islands. Although it is not open to the public, the garden stands as a verdant reminder to Chicagoans of the environmental responsibility everyone faces in the future.

"The erection of a new municipal hall is always an epoch in the history of a city. In the building we are dedicating today we expect will be administered the government of America's greatest city."
Edward J. Brundage
(Corporation Counsel at City Hall dedication, July 20, 1909)

County Clerk Richard J. Daley administers the Oath of Office to Martin H. Kennelly, Chicago's 47th Mayor. (1947-1955)

Federal Judge Abraham Lincoln Marovitz administers the Oath of Office to Chicago's 48th Mayor Richard J. Daley. (1955-1976)

The exterior of the entrance to Chicago's City Hall on LaSalle Street. The four stone reliefs at the doors are by artist John Flanagan. Courtesy of the Chicago History Museum photo archive, CHi-061616.

The Chamber of the Chicago City Council. DN-0009423, courtesy of Chicago History Museum.

Flames shoot from windows of the Chicago City Council Chamber at City Hall, March 22, 1957. Photo courtesy of Rev. John McNalis, 2009.

Political Personalities and Characters in Chicago's City Hall

"One of the penalties for refusing to participate in politics is that you end up being governed by your inferiors"
Plato

Edmund Burke, the Irish political philosopher, wrote—*In politics there are no permanent friends or permanent enemies—only permanent interests.* Nowhere in the nation has that been more true than in Chicago. It has always been the people of Chicago who truly shaped our city's contours and invigorated its soul.

The political character of Chicago continues to dominate our living, carved out of loyalties that never die and alliances that endure from one generation to the next. Like Major League Baseball, it commands our attention and never disappoints. It is the glue of local living.

From Rogers Park to Woodlawn and from South Shore to Austin, the real secret of our urban vitality rests in the most celebrated grid of local communities anywhere.

In our neighborhoods, the pace and proportions of urban life are made manageable. In our neighborhoods we find a place to call our own.

The *New York Times* recently called Chicago – "America's kitchen." It is correct. We are. For in the heartland of the nation, Chicago is America's soul.

It is no exaggeration to say that Chicago is the most American of American cities.

It was Chicago's syndicated 19th century columnist Finley Peter Dunne, the Mike Royko of his day, who was fond of using a famous Chicago observation—*Politics ain't beanbag*; voicing an idea to the rest of the nation that Chicagoans always knew instinctively. Politics in Chicago always has been serious business. Of course, it always has been about the everyday details of municipal governance. But it did not summon the faint of heart. It was tough work; a muscular, brawny and, occasionally, cerebral enterprise.

Politicians have had a remarkable impact on the life of Chicago. Despite their original places of birth, Chicago's politicians easily absorbed the ethos of Chicago life, especially those with a commercial impact on the fast-growing metropolis. Often, Chicagoans who made large contributions to the business and economic life of the city saw their civic influence as critical to safeguarding the important commercial life of Chicago. Over the decades as the numbers and terms of office of members of the City Council evolved, some of America's most colorful political personalities seemed as if they arose from the very soil of the prairie. Many appeared tailor-made for the rough-and-tumble life of the city that was the gateway to the American West. Remarkably, despite their excesses and, often, questionable enterprises, they still managed to represent that most sacred of Chicago interests—their constituents. Many maintained elaborate fiefdoms bolstered by an army of personal political loyalists. Others found that there was simply no limit to the shenanigans that were to be had as a part of local life.

We live in another age of political reality. Where each thought and each misstep are exaggerated by the media. We have endured fresh terrors and new fears in a nation tired of ideology and hungry for hope. So we are proud that here in Chicago we have a unique national political perspective capable of reminding us of American idealism and what change it can create. No longer do opportunities for clout driven armies of political muscle exist. For the most part it is beneficial to be scrutinized by the media and its attention to what is hidden in the shadows redeems the present more than it can constrain it.

We live in a world which Ed Kelly and Richard J. Daley and other big city bosses would find uncomfortable. Our world is by necessity more transparent, more open and more diverse. But we still live in a City that shapes the political world around us locally and nationally.

For Chicagoans politics is ultimately about the delivery of services. People want the traffic to flow; the trash collected; the snow removed and the alleys well lit. Municipal governance is about bringing quality and service to people's lives—neighborhood by neighborhood and house by house.

Politics in Chicago has always been the coin of the realm. It is substantive and effective—"It ain't beanbag." But it is also constantly changing and evolving—if it did not it would cease to exist.

Some Chicago politicians really were transformed by the energy and accomplishment of Chicago elective office and have assisted in the amazing transition of Chicago into the most vibrant city in America.

We must make the world we live in work for our times. But within that we need to be inspired. We will always need to recognize a part of ourselves in those who lead, catching a glimpse of what it is possible for us to become. But is it not more difficult to see the larger paths to hope when the smoke from burning books and burning crosses clog the road before us? Is it not more difficult to see where we are going when we are worried about the strength of our national civility and the protection of our own civil rights? How do we make progress when the diversity in which we live is not reflected in the diversity by which we are governed?

Remarkably, all of this political enterprise has had the luxury and the efficiency of a world-class structure in which to carry out the political debate and strategies for legislation and governance–thanks to the genius and design of Mr. Holabird and Mr. Roche.

*"History is—An echo of
the past in the future; a reflex
from the future on the past."*
Victor Hugo

Aldermen Jacob Arvey, "Bathhouse John" Coughlin (3rd and 4th from left) and other Aldermen await the arrival of a political dignitary at Chicago's Union Station in the 1920's

John D. Caton, 3rd Ward Alderman (1837-1839), was born in March 19, 1812 in Monroe, New York, and attended Utica Academy in New York where he later taught on the faculty. While teaching, he studied law and civil engineering under prominent Utica attorneys. In 1833, he moved to Chicago where he obtained a license to practice law and opened the town's first law office. Caton was elected Alderman of the 3rd Ward in 1837 while he continued to work at his rapidly growing law firm. But as his practice grew, the heavy workload began to take toll on his health. From 1838-1842 he convalesced to regain his health.

When Justice Thomas Ford of the Illinois Supreme Court was elected governor, Caton succeeded him on the State's highest court. He served there for 22 years, becoming Chief Justice in 1855 and again in 1857, retaining the position until his retirement in 1864.

Dr. Josiah Goodhue, 1st Ward Alderman, (1837-1839), was elected in 1837 when Chicago was first incorporated as a City making him the first Alderman to ever represent the 1st Ward of the City. Goodhue, a graduate of the Yale Medical School, was a practicing physician and responsible for designing the first city seal, as well as credited with being the creator of Chicago's first free public school system. Alderman Goodhue died in 1847 when he accidentally fell into a well and drowned.

George Washington Dole, 6th Ward Alderman, (1842-1844), was one of the electors who originally proposed the incorporation of the town of Chicago as a city. His arrival in Chicago coincided with his military service, serving in the Black Hawk War as a First Lieutenant. Dole may be responsible for Chicago's beginnings in the meat packing business when he placed an order for 550 head of cattle to be butchered, packed and sold for military use. Dole was later a member of Chicago's Board of Trustees. On September 4, 1833 the Board of the City elected Dole to be the City's Treasurer. He was a member of the Whig party and ran for mayor in 1844, but was defeated by the incumbent Augustus

Garrett by just seven votes out of 1,796. Although he was unsuccessful in his campaign for mayor, his nephew, Julius S. Rumsey, was elected to the office in 1861, the same year that Abraham Lincoln became President of the United States of America.

John H. Kinzie, 6th Ward Alderman, (1839-1840), came to Chicago in 1804 where he resided until 1812 when he and his family fled to Detroit, escaping the Fort Dearborn Massacre. Kinzie returned to Chicago in 1816 and worked for a fur trading company. He later became Chicago's second town president. On May 2, 1837, he ran against William B. Ogden in the first Mayoral election in Chicago, but lost by a vote of 479 to 220. He went on to become Alderman of the 6th Ward in 1839. Later in life, Kinzie was appointed Registrar of Public Lands by President Harrison in 1841; Canal Collector in 1848; and paymaster in the Army by President Lincoln in 1861 with the rank of major. Kinzie died suddenly on a railroad train on June 21, 1865.

Francis Sherman, 1st Ward Alderman (1837-1838); 5th Mayor (1841-1842) and 23rd Mayor (1862-1863, 1863-1865), was born on September 18, 1805 in Newton, Connecticut. He moved to Chicago in April, 1834, and found work as a brick manufacturer and real estate developer. He accumulated vast wealth in his trade and constructed the City Hotel in 1837 which became the oldest hotel in continuous operation in the State of Illinois until it closed in 1973. Throughout the years it would beknown as the Sherman House. Sherman was elected a village trustee in 1835 while continuing to work as a contractor and builder, and served three terms as mayor from 1841 to 1842; 1862 to 1863, and 1863-1865, the last being the first two year term ever served by a Chicago mayor. His son, Francis Trowbridge Sherman, would become a brigadier general in the Union Army during the American Civil War. The Sherman House was a meeting place for Chicago aldermen, often the scene of clandestine meetings, intrigues and power shifts for more than a century and a half.

Alderman John H. Kinzie
(1839-1849)

Alderman George W. Dole
(1838-1839, 1842-1844)

Alderman Monroe Heath
(1874-1876)

Alderman Josiah C. Goodhue
(1837-1838)

7th Ward Alderman
John N. Kimball chairs a
committee meeting at
City Hall, March 6 1916.
DN-0065867, *Chicago Daily
News* negatives collection,
Chicago History Museum.

Alderman Patrick F. Ryan,
18th Ward (1923-1929) and
politicians Martin Costello
and George Hurst during the
Democratic National Convention
in New York. June 23, 1924.
DN-0076968, *Chicago Daily
News* negatives collection,
Chicago History Museum.

Chicago's patrician
Mayor Carter Harrison II,
Chicago History Museum,
i20086.

Levi D. Boone, 1st Ward Alderman, (1846-1847), and 17th Mayor (1855-1856) was the great-nephew of American pioneer Daniel Boone and a leading member of the *Know-Nothing* political party in Chicago. The *Know-Nothings* were a political party exclusively formed of American-born, Yankee Protestants intolerant of Roman Catholics, immigrants and naturalized U.S. foreign-born citizens, despite their official status. Ironically, at the time, about half of the Chicago's residents were foreign born citizens. He was elected Mayor in 1855. Boone created Chicago's first full-time police department, organized along *Know-Nothing* values, excluding all foreign born citizens and firing all naturalized U.S. citizens employed by the city. He also imposed laws that prohibited the opening of taverns on Sundays and raised the price of liquor licenses. This, in turn, led to the famous Lager Beer Riots in which protesters battled police at the Clark Street Bridge nearby the Cook County Courthouse. Boone was defeated by Thomas Dyer in 1856 which ended the *Know-Nothing's* political influence in Chicago. The election of Dyer also brought an end to Boone's political career. Later, during the Civil War he was arrested as a spy and jailed. He was only released on the express wish of President Lincoln.

James Woodworth, 2nd Ward Alderman, (1845-1846), arrived in Chicago in 1833 the same year Chicago became incorporated as a city. His political career began in 1839 as a State Senator, an office he held until 1842 when he entered the Illinois House of Representatives. He was then elected Alderman of the 2nd Ward. After leaving the House, Woodworth was elected mayor of the City of Chicago following a landslide victory. After serving two consecutive terms as mayor he went on to the United States House of Representatives from Illinois' Second District. During his time as mayor, Woodworth had a municipal sewage system constructed in Chicago, developed in the aftermath of a flood that caused severe freezing in the city's water system. Woodworth was an Independent Republican who was known for his bi-partisanship and his ability to

mediate between the two parties during the Civil War. His legacy lives on in Chicago through many institutions and historical landmarks.

Amos G. Throop, 4th Ward Alderman, (1849-1853), was known for being a devoted abolitionist. Throop, City Treasurer at the time of the Great Fire of 1871, made two unsuccessful attempts to become the Chicago's mayor. He was a member of the Temperance Party that stood in opposition to the Democratic Party. Throop was responsible for helping to secure loans from New York banks for the rebuilding of Chicago in the aftermath of the Fire. The City showed its thanks by renaming Main Street as Throop Street. He later moved to California where he became the Mayor of Pasadena. Throop is also credited with establishing the California Institute of Technology.

"Long" John Wentworth, a graduate of Dartmouth College and owner editor of the *Chicago Democrat*, served as Chicago's 19th and 21st Mayor. Wentworth stood at a colossal 6 ft. 6 in. tall and weighed more than 300 hundred pounds. He was a no-nonsense mayor who attempted to clean up the city, especially the cesspool of saloons and houses of prostitution. He deputized large groups of citizens who assisted him in pulling down whole areas of corruption and crime, like the waterfront denizen known as the Sands. He favored the use of chain gangs and other forms of tough punishment. Ironically, Wentworth drank a pint of whiskey a day. Both a street and pastry are named for him.

It has also been said that this enormous man would consume some 40 different types of food at one meal. Wentworth, a close personal friend of Abraham Lincoln, is responsible for orchestrating the scheme to get "Honest Abe" the Republican nomination for President in 1860. Wentworth resided in a country estate located in what is today known as the Garfield Ridge neighborhood of Chicago. In addition to serving two terms as mayor, Wentworth also served in the United States House of Representatives. A 72-foot-tall obelisk at

Amos G. Throop, 4th Ward Alderman (1849-1853) City Treasurer during the Great Fire of 1871.

Mayor "Long John" Wentworth, 19th, 21st (1857-1858, 1860-1861)

Alderman James H. Woodworth, 12th (1848-1849, 1849-1850)

Workers stand cheering in front of City Hall during a clerk's strike. 1920. DN-0072125, *Chicago Daily News* negatives collection, Chicago History Museum.

9th Ward Alderman Sheldon W. Govier and 4th Ward Alderman David R. Hickey. 1918. DN-0070379, *Chicago Daily News* negatives collection, Chicago History Museum.

Rosehill Cemetery, the tallest monument located within any private cemetery in Chicago recalls his legacy.

John Comiskey, 10th Ward Alderman (1859-1863) and 7th Ward Alderman (1864-1870), Comiskey was an Irish immigrant from County Cavan who arrived in Chicago in 1852. He was the father of Charles A. Comiskey (1859-1931), the founder of the Chicago White Sox. Comiskey remains a name sacred in Chicago sports circles. John Comiskey was the first president of the Chicago Board of Aldermen and also served as Clerk of the Cook County Board, as well as Deputy County Treasurer. Personable, handsome and articulate, he was one of five Irish-born Chairmen of the Chicago City Council Committee on Finance, serving in that post from 1862 to 1865. He gained much public notoriety when he signed a petition calling for Irish volunteers to fight in the American Civil War. He and his colleagues endured much criticism during the Democratic National Convention in Chicago in 1864 when they supported the party's "Copperhead" position that was pro-Southern and called for a quick end to the war in opposition to the policies of President Lincoln. He sat in the Chicago City Council for a total of eleven years and died in 1900.

George Bell Swift, 11th Ward Alderman (1879-81 and 1892-1894) and Mayor (1893, 1895-1897) was born in Cincinnati, Ohio in 1845. His family later moved to Galena, Illinois while he was still young and later settled in Chicago in his teenage years. He served as alderman for two terms beginning in 1879 and was the Commissioner of Public Works from 1887 to 1889. He became Mayor Pro Tempore on November 6, 1893, following the assassination of Mayor Carter Harrison, II. With the mayor's desk and chair heavily draped in black, almost every aldermen attended the council meeting the day following Harrison's death to begin the process of electing an interim replacement. Many Democratic aldermen were at first wary of Swift, being a Republican from the "land of

the buckeyes," but it was soon acknowledged that he was "one of the sort of men that have made Chicago what it is," and he received the majority vote from the City Council. Although he lost his mayoral reelection to John Patrick Hopkins, he regained the mayoral seat in 1895.

Aldermen Michael "Hinky-Dink" Kenna (1897-1923) and **"Bathhouse" John Coughlin** (1893-1938) both represented the 1st Ward in the area that is today in the vicinity of Congress Parkway and Clark Street. Until 1923, each Chicago Ward had two aldermen. At the time there was no shortage of less refined, street-wise Irish politicians in Chicago. No one performed that job better than Kenna and Coughlin did for the very roughest and roguish piece of Chicago geography.

Kenna is believed to be the true author of the saying— "Politics ain't beanbag." Kenna really meant it. He saw politics as a rough and tough endeavor. Despite their scandalous reputations— Kenna and Coughlin were sturdy allies to any mayor willing to make common cause with them— even reformers. In the Levee —the 1st Ward—it was said everyone was on the "take" and unsuspecting tourists rarely escaped a visit to a saloon there without loosing either their money or trousers; or without sampling a "Mickey Finn"—a cocktail with a knockout—invented in Chicago. No political shenanigan was beyond the boys of the Levee. A favorite trick of the aldermen was saved for Election Day. If they suspected a voter of disloyalty or if they could not count on their support, the voter was usually high-jacked out of town, dumped in a remote region outside the city, with no chance of making it back to the city while the polls were open.

Michael Ryan, 14th Ward Alderman (1882– 1886); 15th Ward Alderman (1874-1875); (1889- 1891); and (1893-1895) was an Irish-born politico back when the lagoon at Lincoln Park Zoo was first opening. When it was suggested to the Chicago City Council that the City pay for twelve gondolas for use on the waterway, the issue was debated on

Alderman John Comiskey 10th Ward (1859-1863), 7th Ward (1863-1865), 8th Ward (1867-1869), 9th Ward (1869-1870)

Alderman George Bell Swift, Mayor (1893, 1895-1897). 11th Ward Alderman (1879-1881, 1892-1894)

Alderman Patrick Murray 15th Ward

19th Ward Alderman John Powers (1905-1923), stands in front of his home at 1284 W. Lexington, that was bombed on the night of September 28th, 1920. DN-0072434, *Chicago Daily News* negatives collection, Chicago History Museum.

William H. Sexton, Corporation Counsel, 1911, DN-0009140, *Chicago Daily News* negatives collection, Chicago History Museum.

Alderman "Bath House" John Coughlin, the infamous Alderman of the 1st Ward, 1892-1938. 1909. DN-0054054, *Chicago Daily News* negatives collection, Chicago History Museum.

Judge Otto Kerner, Alderman of the 12th Ward, father of Illinois Governor Otto Kerner, 1917. DN-0068349, *Chicago Daily News* negatives collection, Chicago History Museum.

GIRL SHOOTS ALDERMAN AT CITY HALL

F. M'DERMOTT HIT IN THE LEG; BABY IS CAUSE

Council Startled as Member Drops on the Stairs with Bullet in Limb.

WOMAN TELLS STORY.

She Is Held for Shooting Him.

MRS. ANNA ZIPPMAN M'DERMOTT

FRANK M'DERMOTT

Mrs. Anna Zippman McDermott, accused of shooting her husband, Alderman Frank McDermott, 29th Ward (1910-1916) in City Hall during a City Council meeting. January 26, 1915. DN-0064026. *Chicago Daily News* negatives collection, Chicago History Museum.

16th Ward Alderman Stanley Kunz (1898-1906), sitting in front of a bookcase. 1919. DN-0071289, *Chicago Daily News* negatives collection, Chicago History Museum.

Chicago's first African American Alderman Oscar De Priest of the 2nd Ward (1915-1917). Chicago History Museum, i18381.

13th Ward Alderman Frank McDonald (1912-1914). January 10, 1914. DN-0061952, *Chicago Daily News* negatives collection, Chicago History Museum.

R.A. Bonnell,
City Engineer. 1909.
DN-0007937, *Chicago Daily News* negatives
collection, Chicago
History Museum.

Corporation Counsel
Edward J. Brundage, later
Illinois Attorney General,
1917-1921 and President
of the Cook County Board of
Commissioners. 1905.
DN-0002673, *Chicago Daily News* negatives collection,
Chicago History Museum.

the floor. Ryan addressed the assembly and made a pertinent suggestion. *Why,* said the alderman in his signature Irish brogue, *was it necessary for the city to spend so much on twelve gondolas? Sure couldn't they just buy two and let nature take its course?* As usual his words added both wisdom and humor to Council proceedings. Ryan arrived in Chicago in 1866 after completing his education in Ireland. In addition to representing the 14th and 15th Wards, he served as the Clerk of Cook County.

Oscar De Priest, 2nd Ward Alderman (1915-1917), is not only known as the first African American Alderman in the City of Chicago, but he is also celebrated as the as the first African American to be elected to Congress in the 20th century. Born in Florence, Alabama to former slaves in 1871, De Priest experienced firsthand the hardships in the post war south. In 1878, the De Priest family, along with thousands of other black residents, moved to Kansas in the hopes of escaping the poor economic and social conditions that arose when former Confederates regained control of southern states after Reconstruction. Following graduation from the Salina Normal School with a degree in bookkeeping, he moved to Chicago in 1889 and worked as an apprentice plasterer, house painter and decorator, eventually establishing his own real estate firm.

As the African American population in Chicago grew, De Priest recognized an opportunity for advancing in an area with few Black political leaders. Working behind the scenes at first, he eventually took an active and prominent role in helping the Republican Party, the party of Lincoln, gain influence in the city. He was so successful in delivering the Black vote in the Second and Third Wards that by 1904, he won his first elected position, serving on the Cook County Board of Commissioners. He held this position for two terms until 1908, when he failed to win reelection for a third term.

Taking a break from politics, he focused his attention to his real estate business, helping black families move into formerly all white neighborhoods and becoming an affluent businessman in the process. Deciding to make a return to

politics in 1915, De Priest, aided by favors from powerful Republicans figures, like Mayor William Hale Thompson and Representative Martin Madden. De Priest was elected the first African American Alderman in the Chicago City Council.

As Alderman of the 2nd Ward, De Priest was a spokesperson for the unrepresented Blacks in his community, but he was forced to resign in 1917 after allegations were made about his accepting money from a gambling establishment. De Priest was acquitted of all charges, but failed to gain the endorsement for re-nomination from the Republican Party. He lost the election of 1918 as an Independent.

De Priest entered the national political scene in 1928, when incumbent Congressman Martin Madden died. The Republican Party selected De Priest to replace him on the ballot. He won the election after securing much support from the Black voters in the district. He served three terms as the Representative for the First Congressional District of Illinois, and remained the only African American in Congress during that time. Upon his death both the City Hall and County buildings were closed in a tribute to De Priest.

William Rodriguez, 15th Ward Alderman (1915-1918), was born in Naperville, Illinois and raised in Wisconsin. Rodriguez was part Mexican and part German, but considered himself a true German Socialist. He unsuccessfully ran for mayor of Chicago in 1911, finishing in third place against Mayor Carter Harrison II. Rodriguez was resilient. He went on to successfully campaign for a seat in City Council as Alderman of the 15th Ward. In 1915, Rodriguez became the first Hispanic Alderman in the history of the Chicago City Council.

Joseph McDonough, 5th Ward Alderman, (1917-1923), was a three hundred pound, six-foot-three former football player at Villanova University, and just twenty-eight years old, when he was elected to the City Council from the

William B. Burke,
City Gas Inspector in his
City Hall office. 1908.
DN-0005845, *Chicago Daily
News* negatives collection,
Chicago History Museum.

Aldermen H.C. Knoke,
George Beidley, John M.
Smyth sitting in the City Hall
Council Chamber. 1906.
DN-0004299, *Chicago Daily
News* negatives collection,
Chicago History Museum

15th Ward Alderman William E. Rodriguez, (1915-1918) Chicago's first Hispanic Alderman, February 24, 1916. DN-0065904, *Chicago Daily News* negatives collection, Chicago History Museum.

Aldermen Carl Murray, 18th Ward, Ellis Geiger, 21st, and Jane Addams. July 22, 1915. DN-0064812, *Chicago Daily News* negatives collection, Chicago History Museum.

lace-curtain Irish enclave of Bridgeport. The ultimate political pragmatist, he made common cause with the Bohemian-born future Chicago Mayor Anton Cermak—the man who invented machine politics in Chicago. McDonough's political power greatly increased when he crossed the ethnic line. His political muscle grew when Cermak was elected President of the Cook County Board in 1922, and those ties brought much advantage through the leverage of the patronage system. But no single enterprise of McDonough's political career would ever equal his mentoring of young Richard J. Daley, who decades later, would be propelled into the mayor's office. Daley is seen by many as a legacy of McDonough's, having served as his secretary and assistant for many years. When McDonough won the office of Cook County Treasurer in 1930, through Cermak's influence, Daley went along with him as his top aide. McDonough, however, had little time for the details of office, rarely spending much time there. Daley took on the day-to-day heavy-lifting and learned valuable political lessons that would serve him his whole life. McDonough's influence on Daley cannot be underestimated. He died in 1934.

Dorsey Crowe, 42nd Ward Alderman (1923-1962), left the City Council with a mixed legacy after an eventful 39 year career in the 42nd Ward— the Chicago Gold Coast of tony high-rises and town houses. He had unsuccessfully sought a seat as 21st Ward alderman in 1919, but he was thought to be unqualified and without any real political associations. Putting the defeat behind him, he was successful in getting elected in the 42nd Ward in 1923 and went to work right away. Backed by Gold Coast residents, Crowe requested funds to build bathing facilities at the Ohio Street beach in order to relieve the growing congestion of the ever popular lake front location. Crowe soon ran into trouble, however, during the 1924 mayoral election between "Big" Bill Thompson, former alderman of the 2nd Ward, and William Dever, 17th Ward alderman. Thompson's anti-prohibition views and general

tolerance of corruption provided him with the support of Chicago's organized crime, while Dever, who was running on a reform platform, was seen as a threat. Crowe, one of Dever's biggest supporters in the City Council, experienced firsthand resistance from the criminal element when Vincent Drucci, a member of the Northside Gang, made plans to kidnap him on the night before the election. Drucci broke into Crowe's office, but could not locate him, choosing instead to assault his secretary and vandalize his office. The offenders were quickly apprehended on the street and were soon in police custody. While being escorted to the police station, Drucci was shot and killed during a scuffle with a police detective. Years later, in 1930, financial records were found linking Crowe to mobster Jack Zuta, although Crowe claimed any money he had received from Zuta came legally in the form of campaign contributions. Crowe endured these accusations and retained his position as Alderman of the 42nd Ward until his death in 1962. He had been alderman for 39 years. It was said no one in the 42nd Ward could buy so much as a box of matches without his knowing about it.

Jacob M. Arvey, (Colonel) 24th Ward Alderman (1923-1941), was born to Jewish immigrants from Russia and grew up in Chicago's 24th Ward. Without ever attending college, Arvey attended John Marshall School of Law. He later practiced law at several firms, including Arvey, Hodes, Costello & Burman. He was elected to the City Council from his native 24th Ward in 1923 and quickly became the third ranking member of the powerful political machine run by Mayor Ed Kelly. His ability to consistently turn out the largest Democratic majority in any ward contributed to his influence and reputation among political leaders. Relying heavily on the ability of his precinct captains to make personal contact with potential voters, Arvey claimed the secret of his success was "service." *If an apartment was vacant and you moved in, the precinct captain was there to welcome you. He'd get the electricity turned on, perhaps get milk for your children; he'd help with your tax problems,*

Alderman Joseph B. McDonough
5th Ward (1917-1923)

Alderman Dorsey Crowe
42nd Ward (1923-1962)

Alderman John Duffy
19th Ward (1935-1950)
Finance Chair (1947-1950)

Alderman Jacob M. Arvey
24th Ward (1923-1941)
Finance Chair (1935-1941)

James Dalrymple and Mayor Edward Fitzsimmons Dunne standing in front of City Hall. 1906. DN-0003731, *Chicago Daily News* negatives collection, Chicago History Museum.

William Hale Thompson taking mayoral oath of office administered by Francis D. Connery, the City Clerk. April 11, 1915. DN-0064336, *Chicago Daily News* negatives collection, Chicago History Museum.

Former Mayor Edward Fitzsimmons Dunne, became the Governor of Illinois, he was the only person to ever hold both offices, marked with an X, 1908. DN-0006574, *Chicago Daily News* negatives collection, Chicago History Museum.

Mayor William E. Dever standing with a group of civic leaders. 1925. DN-0078436, *Chicago Daily News* negatives collection, Chicago History Museum.

(right to left)
Aldermen Oscar Olson,
15th, Thomas Lynch, 35th,
Robert Mulcahy, 5th,
Thomas Byrne, 29th, and
Scott Hogan, 31st. 1920.
DN-0071713, *Chicago Daily News* negatives collection,
Chicago History Museum.

Alderman Charles E. Merriam,
7th Ward, 1909-1911,
1913-1917, (top of table)
presides at Committee Meeting.
Later ran for Mayor in 1911.
Distinguished professor of
Political Science at the
University of Chicago. 1909.
DN-0007927, *Chicago Daily News* negatives collection,
Chicago History Museum.

Alderman Robert E. Merriam,
5th Ward, 1947-1955,
ran as the Republican
Candidate as Mayor in 1955
against Richard J. Daley.
He was the son of Alderman
Charles E. Merriam.

or garbage. (*Illinois Issues*, November 1977) His strategy was successful, often resulting in nine to one majorities for Democratic candidates.

Arvey took a leave from politics during World War II, serving as a Judge Advocate General of the 33rd Infantry Division in the South Pacific, going on to earn the Bronze Star and Legion of Merit. Upon his return to Chicago, he took on the role of a reformer, spending the rest of his political career attempting to restore the image of the Democratic Party which he saw tarnished by corruption.

Clarence R. Wagner, 14th Ward Alderman (1943-1953), was among Chicago's most powerful and intelligent political leaders, serving as the administration's floor leader in the City Council. A 1925 graduate of DePaul University School of Law, he was a practicing attorney before entering the Chicago City Council. He also served as an Assistant Probate Court Judge in Cook County beginning in 1935 when he was only 31 years old. In 1943 he was elected Alderman of the 14th Ward, a significant piece of Chicago political geography which had established itself as a well-organized and clout-rich bastion of Regular Democratic Party loyalty—a characterization that meant it was faithful to the traditions of Chicago's unwavering Democratic non-reform ethos. Together with the 14th Ward's other loyalist leaders—Judge James J. McDermott (former alderman) and Justice John J. Sullivan, as well as 19th Ward Committeeman Tom Nash—they stood strong against the political forces of the Kelly-Nash-Arvey machine as the race to unseat Mayor Martin Kennelly got underway in the early 1950s. By 1950 Wagner had become a shining star having been elected Chairman of the powerful Chicago City Council Committee on Finance. Wagner was often seen as the "unofficial mayor" because of the leverage he held within City Hall. Some historians speculated that he would have been the candidate to run for Mayor in the post-Kennelly era. Sadly, at the height of his political power Wagner was killed in an automobile accident in International Falls, Minnesota while vacationing with his sons and

Senator Donald J. O'Brien and his sons. His untimely death left a power vacuum which was quickly filled by the Chairman of the Cook County Democratic Organization, Richard J. Daley, who was elected Mayor in 1955.

Joseph Burke, 14th Ward Alderman, (1953-1968) was elected to this important southside seat in 1953—replacing Alderman Clarence Wagner, the powerful Chairman of the Finance Committee. He was a staunch 14th Ward worker and a deputy of the Cook County Sheriff's Office, before he ran for Alderman. The death of Clarence Wagner would ultimately change the Burke family's life intensifying their involvement in Chicago politics. Burke served for 15 years and was a well-respected and pragmatic local leader. He was not a part of Mayor Richard J. Daley's inner circle but was supportive of Daley's initiatives. Joe Burke served as an effective representative of the 14th Ward until his death in May of 1968. He was a hands-on leader; always present at wakes and events of importance in people's lives. He was approachable and true to his word in a community where people knew their neighbors names and their business. Burke was, then, succeeded by his son, Edward, following a special election in April 1969. Edward M. Burke continues serving the City Council—its longest serving member in history.

The Cullertons

No family demonstrated more local political muscle than this vibrant Chicago family—beginning with Edward "Foxy Eddie" Cullerton himself— first elected to the Common Council before the Great Fire. He clocked 41-years there—though not serving continuously or contiguously from the same Ward, representing the 7th, 6th, 9th and 11th Wards over the decades of his career.

"Foxy Eddie" began a dynasty of public service that continues to this day; and over the decades saw Cullerton descendents reinvent their political power and success. John Cullerton, a nephew of Foxy Eddie, served as Chicago Fire Commissioner in the 1920s.

14th Ward stalwart
Justice John J. Sullivan

14th Ward Alderman
Clarence Wagner (1943-1953)
Finance Chair (1950-1953)

Alderman Joseph Burke
14th Ward (1953-1968)

Edward Cullerton, 7th Ward Alderman (1871-1875); 6th Ward (1876-1888); 9th Ward (1888-1892; 1898-1900) and 11th Ward (1901-1920), was a native Chicagoan, born to Irish immigrants on October 11, 1842. Although he had no opportunity for a formal instruction, he obtained a practical business education working in a brickyard, boarding stable, and later as a driver on the Illinois and Michigan Canal, eventually becoming Captain and owner of the boat. In 1871, at the age of 31, Cullerton was elected to the Common Council to represent the 7th Ward, and one year later was elected to the Illinois State Legislature. Over the course of his career he served in four different wards (7th, 6th, 9th, 11th), taking an eight year hiatus to serve in the General Assembly, earning him the title as record holder for City Council longevity until 2009 when 14th Ward Alderman Edward M. Burke surpassed him with 40 years of unbroken service in the Council with election from the same ward. During his tenure, Cullerton adopted a posture of aggressive leadership and assertiveness within the Council Chamber, gaining a reputation as an experienced, capable representative who maintained the support and confidence of people in and out of his ward. He died in 1920 at the age of 79.

No Cullerton did a better job politically than **Alderman Patrick J. "Parky" Cullerton,** 38th Ward Alderman (1935-1958)—the staunch ally of Mayor Richard J. Daley. Parky, like his niece, P.J., served as Committeeman of the 38th Ward. Following Parky's move to the Cook County Assessor's Office, in 1958, his brother, **William J. Cullerton,** (1959-1973) was elected to succeed him as alderman; upon his death, in 1973, his nephew, **Thomas Cullerton,** (1973-1993) was elected to succeed him. Upon his death, 20 years later, he was followed by his protégée, **Thomas R. Allen,** a Cullerton by marriage (1993 to present). Allen recently ran un-successfully for Cook County State's Attorney in 2008.

Despite the dire predictions following Parky Cullerton's death in 1981, the Cullerton Family remained electable and continues to provide re-markable public service. But Parky's passing did mark the finality of old-fashioned politics. Chicago's neighborhoods and Ward organizations reinvented themselves in many areas across the City. New alliances and political relationships took the place of "the old boys network" and ethnic connections. Another family member, Illinois Senator John Cullerton, currently serves as President of the Illinois State Senate.

John Powers, 19th Ward Alderman (1905-1923), was a saloon keeper and a craftsman in political corruption. Many reformers tried to unseat Alderman Powers during his years in office, including Nobel Laureate Jane Addams, the founder of Hull House. During the Aldermanic election of 1921 large-scale violence erupted in Chicago mainly within the 19th Ward where the incumbent, Powers, was facing off against a candidate named Anthony d'Andrea. Several bombings occurred at the headquarters of different precincts within the 19th Ward, including Powers own home on Lexington Avenue. D'Andrea was a defrocked priest who swore he would reform the city. During the election, the media and d'Andrea constantly attacked Powers credibility as a public official and labeled him as corrupt. Powers won the election and shortly afterwards d'Andrea was murdered by assassins carrying sawed-off shotguns.

John S. Clark Jr., 30th Ward Alderman (1917-1934), was erudite and a distinguished Brahman already, when he was elected Alderman in 1917 at 25 years of age. In 1927 he became Chairman of the powerful Chicago City Council Committee on Finance. He would serve in the City Council until 1934 when he was elected the Assessor of Cook County, a post he held for 20 years. He was the son of Alderman John S. Clark, of the 35th Ward (1909-1911) and the father of Illinois Supreme Court Justice William G. Clark (1976-1992). The Clarks were a prominent Westside Irish dynasty of refined political abilities. Clark Park at 4615 W. Jackson Boulevard is named in his honor.

Alderman Edward F. Cullerton 7th Ward (1871-1875), 6th Ward (1876-1888), 9th Ward (1888-1892; 1898-1900), 11th Ward (1901-1920)
38th Ward Aldermen: Patrick J. "Parky" Cullerton (1935-1958), Finance Chair (1953-1958)
William J. Cullerton (1959-1973)
Thomas Cullerton (1973-1993)

Terrance Moran, 16th Ward Alderman (1923-1939), was known as one of the less efficient members of the Finance Committee, but still managed to serve the 16th Ward for 16 years. When Queen Marie of Romania toured the United States in 1926, she became a small celebrity. That attention eroded when she made a four day stop in Chicago. Many aldermen were reluctant to be seen meeting with an autocrat royal two months before the upcoming election. When Moran was asked if he was planning to attend the City Hall reception, he told reporters "I lived in Ireland, and the tyranny of the kings and queens was one of the reasons why I left. There's hundreds of thousands who hold the same view. Count me out." Only seven out of fifty aldermen attended the ceremony in honor of Queen Marie—a granddaughter of Queen Victoria of England.

Joseph Rostenkowski, 32nd Ward Alderman (1933-1955), or "Joe Rosty" as he was better known, became a classic ward boss following his election in 1933, though without the usual scandal or corruption. Gaining power through strong personal relationships with his constituents and unwavering loyalty to the Democratic Party organization, he quickly established himself as the leader of the "Polish Downtown," the area near Milwaukee Avenue, Ashland and Division Streets that was home to more Poles anywhere outside of Warsaw. Throughout the depression years when residents were out of work, Rostenkowski's ward distributed food and coal baskets and helped pay gas and electric bills. His unparalleled involvement with his constituents was well rewarded. Joe's son, Dan, a powerful Congressman and for many years Chairman of the House Ways and Means Committee, often told a story that when Polish immigrants from the 32nd Ward were asked on their citizenship test who was the President of the United States, many would answer with the name Joseph Rostenkowski.

The Keanes—

Thomas P. Keane, 31st Ward Alderman (1933-1945), this Keane was the father of Thomas E. Keane and began the family's stronghold of the Humboldt Park community's political influence and control.

Thomas E. Keane, 31st Ward Alderman (1945-1974), was Mayor Richard J. Daley's longtime loyalist and floor leader in the City Council. Keane was a member of the Illinois State Senate at the time of his father's death in 1945 and stepped in to take his place running in the special election to fill his seat in the City Council. As an influential Ward Committeeman, he was part of the efforts in the Cook County Democratic Central Committee to unseat Mayor Martin Kennelly in 1954. Democratic leaders in turn slated the Chairman of the Cook County Democratic Central Committee, Richard J. Daley, to run in 1955 for Mayor. Keane has often been characterized as Daley's closet political ally who ruled the Council on Daley's behalf with an iron fist. In 1958 Keane became Chairman of the Committee on Finance, the Council's most powerful position. Following a grueling investigation by the *Chicago Sun-Times*, the federal government indicted Keane. He was subsequently convicted in 1974 of some eighteen counts of federal mail fraud and conspiracy. Later, the United States Supreme Court overturned his conviction, and the Illinois Supreme Court restored his law license.

Adeline Keane, 31st Ward Alderman (1975-1979), was the political neophyte wife of Alderman Thomas E. Keane who succeeded her husband upon his conviction in 1974. She was slated by her husband and took the seat that would be in the family for more than forty-six years. Even beyond this, Tom Keane's maternal grandfather and uncle served as aldermen as well.

Roman C. Pucinski, 41st Ward Alderman (1973-1991), spent 14 years in the U.S. House of Representatives before entering the Chicago City

Alderman John S. Clark, Jr.
30th Ward (1917-1934)
Finance Chairman (1927-1935)

Alderman James B. Bowler
19th Ward (1906-1923)
25th Ward (1927-1953)
Finance Chairman (1941-1947)

Alderman Thomas P. Keane
31st Ward (1933-1945)
Finance Chairman (1958-1974)

Mayor Richard M. Daley
with Alderman Thomas R. Allen
(1993-present)

Mayor "Big Bill" Thompson celebrates his victorious return to the Office of Mayor (during prohibition) in his usual zanny manner, surrounded by his cadre of Chicago characters. Chicago wasn't ready for reform. April 5 1927. DN-0083307, *Chicago Daily News* negatives collection, Chicago History Museum.

Council after an unsuccessful run for the U.S. Senate in 1972 against Senator Charles Percy. Pucinski was an aristocratic and erudite political leader within Chicago's large Polish Community, as well as a highly decorated U.S. Air Force veteran in World War II. In the Council he was part of the "Vrdolyak 29" during the administration of Mayor Harold Washington. Among the mundane issues important to Chicago life that he championed were those concerning Employee Stock Ownership and the redistribution of Community Development Grants. But he will always be remembered for his leadership in Congress where he helped to secure the installation of the "Black Box" flight recorders on all passenger airliners.

Leon Depres, 5th Ward Alderman (1955-1975), was a "political independent" who arrived in the Chicago City Council just when Richard J. Daley was elected mayor. He represented the ward in which the prestigious University of Chicago is located. His constituents were poor African Americans, as well as Nobel Laureates, scientists, physicists and intellectuals of every persuasion. He was a well-established Chicago lawyer when he was elected in an era when political independence was not highly regarded, especially in the Chicago City Council. He was Jewish, wealthy, advantaged, sophisticated, well travelled, a patron of the arts and a champion of the under class. He was a friend of the celebrated Mexican painter, Diego Rivera, and his artist wife, Frieda Kahlo. As a young, wealthy socialist in the 1930s, Depres travelled to Mexico to assist Leon Trotsky after he fled the Soviet Union and sought refuge in Mexico. Depres is said to have given Trotsky all his clothes since they were the same size, very tall and skinny. Rivera painted his wife, Marian Depres', portrait at the time. Depres came to the City Council a renaissance man and for all those years stood proud, and a little frustrated, by the more popular political opinions of the day. Remarkably he outlasted his critics and opponents living passed 100. He had no stronger critic than Mayor Richard J. Daley who had little time for his fancy politics or

intellectual theories. Daley continuously and bitterly rebuked his reformist tendencies. He came to the Chicago City Council a champion for his people and never retreated from an unpopular cause or an unpopular idea. He came from a unique world of ideas—always bright, fresh and undaunting. Depres was filled with an aristocratic tenacity and courage, unwavering in the face of, often, tremendous opposition. He never seemed to fear the power or the might that was frequently staring down at him. He brought character to the City Council and an elegant sense of political refinement. He died in 2009 at the age of 101.

Seymour Simon, 40th Ward Alderman (1955-1961; and 1967-1974), was one of the few Chicago citizens to have the opportunity to serve in all three branches of government. He served as the Alderman of the 40th Ward in the legislative branch; then as President of the Cook County Board in the executive branch; and then as both an Appellate and Supreme Court Justice in the judicial branch. His career was characterized by a strong sense of patriotism and commitment to the law. He took to heart Thomas Jefferson's great admonition—"Determine never to be idle." His unpopular support of a motion for open housing in 1961, though soundly defeated, initiated the debate and the dialogue that would pave the way for its later triumph. His fight for open housing truly illustrated how fairness and opportunity in every aspect of human life was always at the heart of who he was as a person.

Theris "Terri" Gabinski, 32nd Ward Alderman (1969-1999), a former high school chemistry teacher, was elected and then sworn in on the same day as fellow aldermen Edward M. Burke, (14th Ward) and Fred Hubbard (2nd Ward) in 1969, and would go on to serve as Alderman of the 32nd Ward for 30 consecutive years. As a protégé of the powerful Congressman Dan Rostenkowski, a former 32nd Ward Committeeman, Gabinski was an influential force behind the development of his ward, especially in the Bucktown and Lakeview

Alderman Vito Marzulo
25th Ward (1953-1985)

Alderman Roman C. Pucinski
41st Ward (1973-1991)

Alderman Leon Despres
5th Ward (1955-1975)

Alderman Seymour Simon
40th Ward (1955-1961, 1967-1974)

Miss Ruth Harsley, standing behind a tripod camera takes a photo and draws a crowd in front of City Hall. March 20, 1915. DN-0064197, *Chicago Daily News* negatives collection, Chicago History Museum.

areas. Gabinski was a known opponent of the late Mayor Harold Washington, who led the ouster of Gabinski from his position as Chairman of the Zoning Committee in 1987, a seat he had held since 1983. A member of the "Vrdolyak 29" and a Rostenkowski loyalist, Gabinski retired in 1999 and was replaced by former Alderman Ted Matlak. Gabinski remained the 32nd Ward's Democratic Committeeman until 2008 when he was replaced by Illinois State Representative John Fritchey.

Wilson Frost, 21st Ward Alderman (1967-1971) and 34th Ward Alderman (1971-1986), will be remembered as the man who almost became the first African American mayor in the City of Chicago. Born in Cairo, Illinois in 1925, he earned a bachelors degree from Fisk University and later attended the Kent College of Law, earning a J.D. in 1958. After working as a partner for several law firms, including Frost, Sherard, Howse & Coleman; as well as Frost & Greenblatt, he became active in City politics. He was elected alderman of the 21st Ward in 1967 and the 34th Ward in 1971, quickly becoming part of the powerful Chicago political machine and serving as the President Pro Tem of the City Council by 1976. Upon the death of Mayor Richard J. Daley that same year, Frost asserted that under existing law, he was acting mayor of Chicago based on his position as the President Pro Tem of the City Council. Initially set to become the first African American mayor of Chicago, the other aldermen disagreed with his assertion of his claim for the post and the keys to Daley's office could not be found. After several closed door meetings, Alderman Michael Bilandic, 11th Ward Alderman, was elected as Acting Mayor for six months until a special election could be arranged. Although he was denied the mayoral seat, Frost was named Chairman of the Finance Committee, a position with more tangible power than that of President Pro Tem. Frost left City Council in 1986 but continued to serve county government until his retirement 1998.

Burton Natarus, 42nd Ward Alderman (1971-2007), was reelected with alacrity for over 30 years. As a graduate of the John F. Kennedy School of Government at Harvard University, and professor of local politics at Loyola University Chicago, he was well equipped to serve the exceptionally busy neighborhoods of the 42nd Ward which include Streeterville, the Gold Coast, the Magnificent Mile, River North and the Loop. First elected in 1971, he quickly went to work addressing the concerns voiced by residents of his ward. Natarus pioneered the City's first handgun legislation in the early 1970s, and more recently, introduced an ordinance to improve maternity leave benefits for new parents employed by the City. In a drive to promote what he called "livable communities," Natarus balanced interests of both greening/environment and growth in the 42nd Ward. He pushed ordinances that made pet owners responsible for cleaning up after their animals and regulated the horse drawn carriages that traveled throughout his ward. He also moved to limit street musicians in the Rush Street area and worked to eliminate 4:00 a.m. liquor licenses. Despite the support he had gathered throughout his aldermanic career, Natarus had developed a strained relationship with the press by 2006 and was known to use vulgar language with reporters at times. After nine consecutive terms and 36 years in the Council, he was defeated in 2007 by Brendan Reilly in his bid for a 10th term.

Michael J. Bilandic, 11th Ward Alderman, (1969-1977), was a graduate of DePaul University School of Law who represented the Bridgeport neighborhood in the City Council. Following the death of Richard J. Daley in 1976, and Wilson Frost's failed attempt to succeed him until a special election could be held, the City Council, announced that Bilandic would serve as the Acting-Mayor. Bilandic then chose to run in the spring of 1977 and was elected Chicago's 49th mayor. However, his time as mayor was short lived. When a severe

14th Ward Aldermen Ed Burke, (1969-present) and 32nd Ward Alderman Terry Gabinski, (1969-1999), came to the Council in a special election in 1968. Private collection.

34th Ward Alderman Wilson Frost (1967-1981) Finance Chair (1977-1987)

42nd Ward Alderman Burton Natarus (1971-2007) Finance Chair (1988-1989)

snow storm paralyzed the city for days in 1979, Bilandic was blamed for the slow response of the City to remove the snow. He was never able to overcome the stigma of the snowfall. Jane Burke Byrne, who had been Commissioner of Consumer Affairs was summarily removed from her position by him, but easily defeated him at the polls. While Bilandic's career in urban government came to an end as Chicago's chief executive, he went on to an impressive career in the Illinois judiciary. He was elected to the Illinois Appellate Court in 1984, and then to the Illinois Supreme Court in 1990 where he served for ten years.

Marilou McCarthy Hedlund, 48th Ward Alderman (1971-1975), was the first woman ever sworn into the Chicago City Council in 1971, beating fellow inductee Anna Langford by a few hours. A former *Chicago Tribune* reporter, Hedlund was known as a strong community activist and employed a one word campaign button—"Alderwoman"—to win a seat on the Council. Her supporters claimed that the presence of the 33-year old candidate would upgrade both the appearance and total intellectual capacity of the council chambers, bringing a new perspective to issues such as pollution, overcrowded housing, and the general feeling of distrust towards the city administration. The election of women to the City Council, some felt, would bring "fewer mystifying decisions by the council, less cigar smoke, more sensible talk, and the resurgence of the old idea that all aldermen are supposed to represent the best interests of both the area they come from and the City as a whole."

Hedlund's male colleagues initially treated her with a sense of guardedness. The day after the election, Deputy Mayor Dave Stahl voiced his concern regarding his first two tasks of the day: installing a new bathroom in the City Council Chamber and ordering a sign that says "Women." Despite the apprehension of others, Hedlund made a name for herself as a passionate

representative of the Uptown-Edgewater neighborhood and as a strong supporter of Mayor Richard J. Daley. Although many had accepted her as a strong-minded, independent and effective politician, Hedlund left the Council after one term to pursue graduate work at the University of Chicago. She later married the Baron Heinrich von Ferstel, a Viennese Hotel Executive. While no longer Alderman Hedland, she did attain a new title—the Baroness von Ferstel.

Anna Langford, 16th Ward Alderman (1971-1975, 1983-1991), was known to Chicagoans as a woman who pushed the limits and made great strides for the female and African American communities of the City. Although she and Marilou McCarthy Hedlund share the title as the first women to be elected as aldermen in the Chicago City Council, Langford was the first African American woman to hold that position. Losing her parents at a young age, she lived with her grandmother until 1933, when she moved to Chicago with her aunt and uncle. After graduating from Hyde Park High School, she attended a trade school and learned a variety of office skills, securing jobs in the Social Security Administration, the Election Commission Office and in the Office of the Secretary of State.

In 1956, Langford obtained her J.D. degree from John Marshal Law School and began a career in civil rights and criminal law, defending civil rights workers and participating in the Rev. Dr. Martin Luther King, Jr.'s Chicago marches. After an unsuccessful aldermanic campaign in 1967, she went on to defeat George Boggan in 1971 to become the Alderman of the 16th Ward. Using her experience as an established attorney and civil rights advocate, she quickly gained a reputation for integrity and for being a "thorn in the side of those in power."

Langford lost her re-election campaign in 1975 but later regained her seat in 1983, serving two more consecutive terms. She stepped down in 1991 when her term ended, but was remembered for her commitment to the Englewood neighborhood.

Alderman Michael J. Bilandic 11th Ward (1969-1977)

Alderman Marilou McCarthy Hedlund 48rd Ward (1971-1975)

Alderman Anna Langford, 16th ward (1971-1975) and Alderman Cliff Kelly 20th Ward (1971-1987)

Striking clothing workers demonstrate in the hallways of City Hall after they attempted to have a labor march. November 10, 1915. DN-0065397, *Chicago Daily News* negatives collection, Chicago History Museum.

Politician Isaac Rothschild, March 7, 1913. DN-0060254, *Chicago Daily News* negatives collection, Chicago History Museum.

Elevator starter Otto A. Thomsen, City Hall employee, holding his clicker. 1925. DN-0079814, *Chicago Daily News* negatives collection, Chicago History Museum.

William J. McCourt,
Superintendent of the Bureau
of Water. 1908. DN-0005568,
Chicago Daily News
negatives collection,
Chicago History Museum.

Joseph F. Peacock,
City Hall worker. 1921.
DN-0072931, *Chicago Daily
News* negatives collection,
Chicago History Museum.

Rev. Jesse Jackson described her as "a beacon of hope that spoke truth to power fearlessly." She was awarded a number of humanitarian and civic awards for her accomplishments and was even inducted into the *Book of Legends* by the Black Women Lawyers Association for her contributions as an attorney and public servant. Langford remained in the Englewood neighborhood and died in 2008 at the age of 90 after a battle with lung cancer.

Timothy C. Evans, 4th Ward Alderman (1973-1991), won his seat in a special election called to fill the vacant seat previously held by Alderman Claude W.B. Holman. In that race Evans defeated Hattie B. Kay Williams, a 50-year old Girl Scout Executive, in a landslide victory. He became Council floor leader in 1983 under Mayor Harold Washington. Evans was later named Chairman of the Council's powerful Finance Committee by Washington. Upon the death of Harold Washington, during the contentious battle for a successor, Evans, appeared a popular candidate for many, and made an effort to express interest in being a candidate for mayor; but was unsuccessful in the special late-night election in which the City Council elected Alderman Eugene Sawyer, of the 6th Ward (1971-1987), to replace Washington and complete his unexpired term as the City's second African American mayor. Evans, later ran in the 1989 mayoral race, but was defeated by Richard M. Daley. Evans now serves as the Chief Judge of the Cook County Circuit Court, the first African American to hold the office.

Edward R. Vrdolyak, 10th Ward Alderman (1971-1987), is a Chicago attorney. He was elected Alderman in 1971 and served as City Council President Pro Tem from 1977 to 1983. He earned his nickname, "Fast Eddie," from his amazing ability to make back room deals. He is most known for his facing off with Mayor Harold Washington in what became characterized as "Council Wars." Vrdolyak, along with 28 other Aldermen known

as the "Vrdolyak 29," voted against all of Washington's appointments, however, they could not override Washington's ability to veto ordinances. Alderman Vrdolyak along with Alderman Edward M. Burke led the 29 Alderman opposing Washington. Council Wars continued until the death of Harold Washington in 1987 when Alderman Eugene Sawyer was elected to replace him.

When a 1986 federal lawsuit brought about substantive political redistricting in Chicago, some of Vrdolyak's staunchest allies were defeated by Washington supporters. Vrdolyak and his allies lost some leverage giving Harold Washington more political control. Vrdolyak later left the Democratic Party and made an unsuccessful attempt running against Harold Washington in the 1987 mayoral election as the Solidarity Party nominee. Vrdolyak's defeat, then, and his later loss in the election in 1988 for Clerk of the Circuit Court of Cook County, were difficult political pills to swallow. Thereafter, he ran for mayor in 1989 as the Republican Party nominee against Richard M. Daley. Vrdolyak received less than 4% of the vote, thus, bringing an end to his political career.

Victor A. Vrdolyak, 10th Ward Alderman (1987-1991), a former Deputy Superintendent for the Chicago Police Department took his younger brother, Edward's, seat as 10th Ward Alderman immediately after his brother left office. In 1991, Victor decided not to seek re-election.

Dick Simpson, 44th Ward Alderman (1971-1979), consistently introduced reform legislation to the Chicago City Council and often succeeded in persuading veteran Aldermen to vote with him. Some of the legislation Simpson produced dealt with issues like more spending for day care and a variety of programs that benefitted the homeless. Simpson led the Council's opposition block to Daley and Bilandic. Mayor Richard J. Daley often left him go unrecognized on the Council floor unable to use his microphone to be heard. He is co-author

Alderman Timothy C. Evans
4th Ward (1973-1991)
Finance Chair (1987-1988)

Alderman Edward R. Vrdolyak
10th Ward (1987-1991)

of sixteen books involving politics and has lived a life of scholarship and academic success. Simpson is currently on the faculty of the University of Illinois in Chicago in the Political Science Department and Chair of the Public Service Committee.

Richard F. "Dick" Mell, 33rd Ward, (1975-present), is Chairman of the influential Committee on Committees, Rules and Ethics and is known for his independent stands. Mell, an ally of the "Vrdolyak 29" during Council Wars, was elected Alderman of the 33rd Ward in 1975. Mell played a pivitol role in son-in-law Rod Blagojevich's successful 2002 gubernational campaign. However, the two began feuding in 2005. Mell has been an important legislator for the city through various legislative initiatives including banning the sale of spraypaint which has successfully curbed the City's neverending war against graffiti. Mell's image was preserved for history standing atop his desk while attempting to get the attention of the bitterly divided City Council during the famous all night meeting on December 2, 1987 to elect a successor to Harold Washington.

Bernard L. Stone, 50th Ward, (1973-present), with 36 years in office, is the second longest serving Alderman in the City Council. He is also the Vice-Mayor of Chicago. His first attempt at elected office was in 1956 when he unsuccessfully ran for a seat in the Illinois House of Representatives. Seventeen years later, Stone was successfully elected alderman of the 50th Ward located in the West Roger's Park neighborhood on Chicago's Northside. Stone was an ally of former Alderman Ed Vrdolyak and a member of the "Vrdolyak 29" during the

Council Wars. Vrdolyak convinced Stone to join the Republican Party in 1987. Although Stone switched parties, he continued to retain his office. Just one month after announcing that he had switched parties, Mayor Harold Washington died of a heart attack and Stone made an unsuccessful attempt to persuade his colleagues to elect him to the post. In 1988 Stone lost against Carol Moseley Braun in a race for Recorder of Deeds. In 1989 he ran for Mayor but was defeated by Richard M. Daley. In 2003 Stone's son ran for Alderman of the 32nd Ward and Stone publically supported his rival, Theodore Matlak.

Dorothy Tillman, 3rd Ward Alderman, (1984-2007), was an activist for Martin Luther King's Southern Christian Leadership Conference and a strong advocate of the Civil Right's movement. Tillman marched with King in the Selma to Montgomery marches, befriending him. As a result of her activism, she got her start in Chicago politics. In 1965, King sent Tillman, who was originally from Alabama, to Chicago to rally for better housing and education for African Americans. She stayed in Chicago for several years, but later left to live with her husband in San Francisco. Upon her return, Tillman was elected Alderman of the 3rd Ward in 1984, the first woman to ever represent it. Tillman became a strong voice for reperations for slavery and often challenged her colleagues in the City Council on the issue. In 2007, Tillman was defeated by her opponent, Pat Dowell. Dorothy Tillman was a colorful and out spoken legislator, not only known for her activism, she is also remembered for her hats. Almost always seen wearing one of over two hundred spectacular hats, they quickly became part of her image, a trademark which she cultivated and established throughout the years.

Alderman Dick Mell
33rd Ward (1975-present)

Alderman Dorothy Tillman,
3rd Ward (1984-2007) and
Alderman William Banks,
36th Ward (1983-2009)

Luis Gutierrez, 26th Ward Alderman (1986-1992), a Chicagoan since birth, has spent much of his career trying to improve the lives of Hispanic immigrants in his community. He gained valuable experience from a number of jobs before his decision to enter politics, working as a teacher, community activist and social worker for the Illinois Department of Children and Family Services. After his election to the Chicago City Council in 1986, he led the fight for affordable housing, tougher ethics rules and a law to ban discrimination based on sexual orientation. In addition to these efforts, Gutierrez established citizenship workshops offering comprehensive assistance to prospective citizens that have helped more than 40,000 people take their first steps towards naturalization. After leaving the City Council, he was elected the first Latino Congressman from the Midwest in 1992, representing Illinois' 4th District where he continues to address the needs of the large Eastern European and Latin American immigrant communities in his diverse district.

Alderman Carrie Austin
34th Ward (1994-to present)

Alderman Ike Carothers
29th Ward (1999-to present)

Alderman Pat Dowell
3rd Ward (2007-to present)

Alderman Luis Gutierrez
26th Ward (1986-1992)

Alderman Sandi Jackson
7th Ward (2007-to present)

Alderman Ginger Rugai
19th Ward (1990-to present)

Alderman Latasha Thomas
17th Ward (2000- to present)

Alderman Tom Tunney
44th Ward (2002-to present)

> *"Liberty means responsibility.*
> *That is why men so dread it."*
> John Kennedy

"Bathhouse John" Coughlin holds Court, (2nd from left in front) and Alderman Thomas P. Keane (seated far right), father of Alderman Thomas E. Keane.

Mayor Richard J. Daley escorts Queen Elizabeth II to dinner during her historic 1959 Chicago visit. Chicago History Museum, i30172.

Mayor Richard J. Daley at his 5th floor desk in Chicago's City Hall. Chicago History Museum, i25429.

Mayor Richard J. Daley and a very young Reverend Jesse Jackson, 1970's. Chicago History Museum, i35614.

Mayor Richard J. Daley rides with Queen Elizabeth II on her arrival near Buckingham Fountain from the Royal yacht, H.M.S. Britannia in 1959. Chicago History Museum, i30171

Mayor Richard J. Daley manning the phone in his 5th floor City Hall office. Chicago History Museum, i25547.

44th Ward Alderman, and University of Illinois faculty member, Dick Simpson, (1971-1979) is restrained by police at his Council seat after Mayor Richard J. Daley ordered him to be seated in 1976. Photo courtesy of professor Richard Simpson archive.

The present Chamber of the Chicago City Council with the cool modernity of the United Nations-style chamber. Courtesy of the Chicago History Museum.

Mayor Kelly with Chicago Aldermen, Chicago business leaders and state elected officials at the opening of the Outer Drive Extension, 1933. Chicago History Museum, i16867.

Holabird & Roche designed the Sherman House across the street from
City Hall in 1911. Chicago History Museum. io0459.

Chicago's Mayors
1907–Present
All Who Served in the Seventh City Hall

Fred A. Busse (39th Mayor, 1907-1911)

Fred Busse was first elected to the Illinois State Legislature in 1894 and served as State Treasurer in 1902. In 1905, President Theodore Roosevelt appointed him the Postmaster of Chicago. Without any campaign appearances or speeches, he still was victorious in the mayoral election of 1907 against Democratic incumbent Edward Fitzsimmons Dunne. Busse's tenure in office was often characterized by extensive corruption. He was the Mayor during the 1908 Republican National Presidential Convention held in the Chicago Coliseum on Wabash Avenue at which William Howard Taft received the nomination. Busse was the first Chicago Mayor elected to a four-year term and was mayor during the construction of Chicago's seventh City Hall. He died of heart disease in 1914, at the age of 48, and was buried at Graceland Cemetery.

Carter Harrison, II (37th Mayor, 1897-1905; 40th Mayor, 1911-1915)

Carter Harrison II had five terms in office as Chicago's mayor; its 37th and its 40th. He was also the son of a Chicago mayor, Carter Harrison I. Educated in Europe, Harrison II was a Chicago aristocrat like his father and had the distinction of being the first Chicago mayor to actually be born in the City. After the senior Harrison purchased the *Chicago Times*, a newspaper supporting Democratic Party initiatives, the younger Harrison returned to Chicago to help run the family newspaper—the only newspaper in town that supported the workers in the Pullman Strike. He was forthright, articulate and intelligent, filled with the ideals of the age. His father, the first mayor to be elected to five terms in office, was assassinated on the eve of the closing of the 1893 World's Columbian Exposition. The younger Harrison himself was elected mayor in 1897. His first four terms in office had none of his father's focus on moral probity, but helped to initiate some of the massive change that came to Chicago in commerce and industry. But after leaving office in 1905, he was returned to office six years later as a reformer. During that 5th term he went to war over vice and disorder,

going so far as to shutter the Everleigh Club, an infamous brothel, as well as closing down the Levee, a near southside neighborhood of crime and shenanigans operated by Aldermen Kenna and Coughlin of the 1st Ward, that ended Harrison's political détente with them.

William Hale "Big Bill Thompson" (41st Mayor, 1915-1923, 43rd Mayor, 1927-1931)

William Hale Thompson was the last Republican to serve as Mayor to Chicago. He was known as a flamboyant campaigner and once held a live debate between himself and two live rats used to portray his opponents. He saw more than his fair share of action while he was in office, with events such as the St. Valentine's Day Massacre, the "Pineapple Primary" and The Chicago Race Riots of 1919 taking place during his three terms as mayor. He welcomed two Republican National Presidential Conventions— 1916, nominating Charles Evans Hughes, and 1920, nominating Warren G. Harding. The unpredictable Thompson once permitted a rodeo to ride their horses into the City Council Chambers. After two terms in office, Thompson was voted out of office. But he re-turned again in 1927 and won handily with the backing of Al Capone and Chicago's Irish voters, thrilled with his "anti-British" rhetoric. Thompson's tenure as Mayor has long been tinged with charges of corruption. Upon his death two safe deposit boxes were found in his name containing nearly $1.5 million in cash. And on his death he was laid-in-state in Chicago's City Hall with the City Council holding a memorial. He was buried at Oak Woods Cemetery where his obelisk is the tallest monument there.

William Emmett Dever (42nd Mayor, 1923-1927)

William Dever served as the 42nd Mayor of Chicago. Before his election as mayor, he was a judge of the Cook County Circuit Court and later served eight years as Alderman of the 17th Ward. In 1923, Democratic Party boss George Brennan selected Dever as the best "reform" candidate to run against two-term incumbent William Hale Thompson. With scandals rampant within the

Mayor Fred A. Busse
Mayor Carter Harrison II
Mayor William Hale Thompson
Mayor William Emmett Dever

Funeral cortege of Mayor Anton Cermak,
May 13, 1933

Thompson administration, "Big Bill" withdrew from the race, allowing Dever to win with ease. Under Dever's leadership, the City saw substantial improvements in its infrastructure, including the completion of Wacker Drive, the expansion of Ogden Avenue, the development of plans to straighten the south branch of the Chicago River and the construction of Chicago's first municipal airport, known today as Midway Airport. He also stood firm against bootleggers and organized crime. With a more aggressive attitude enforcing Prohibition than Thompson, Dever waged war with bootleggers, labeled "the Great Beer War." William Dever ran for re-election in 1927 but lost to a rejuvenated Thompson. Dever died of cancer in 1929 and was buried at Calvary Cemetery in Evanston.

Anton Joseph Cermak (44th Mayor, 1931-1933)
Anton Cermak was born in Bohemia, in the old Austro-Hungarian Empire, and remains Chicago's first and only foreign-born chief executive. Before becoming Chicago's 44th Mayor, Cermak was elected to the Illinois State Legislature, the Cook County Board of Commissioners where he served as president, and served as Chairman of the Cook County Democratic Party. He was also the Alderman of the 12th Ward. Cermak's political and organizational muscle helped to create one of the most vibrant and powerful political organizations in the nation. He is considered the "father" of the Chicago Political Machine. While mayor, Cermak welcomed the 1932 Democratic National Convention that chose Franklin Delano Roosevelt as its presidential candidate and the 1932 Republican National Convention that re-nominated President Herbert Hoover. Because Cermak had not supported Roosevelt in his bid for the nomination, he traveled to mend fences with the president-elect in Miami, Florida. While appearing at an event with Roosevelt, on February 15, 1933, Cermak was shot and seriously wounded by an assassin named Giuseppe Zangara. While some believe that Roosevelt was the target of the Sicilian, others note that Cermak was the target all along because of his antagonism with Chicago mob-boss Frank Nitti.

Cermak died of his wounds weeks later, March 6, 1933. He was waked in City Hall with more than 70,000 people, many of whom waited in the bitter cold, paying their respects. He was buried in Bohemia National Cemetery.

Frank Corr (45th Mayor, 1933)
Few Chicagoans remember Frank Corr. Even fewer recall that he was, once, mayor of the City. Following the death of the Mayor Anton Cermak, Democrats scurried to find a replacement. The odds-on favorite was the President of the South Park Board, Ed Kelly, a man who knew his way around the political machinery of Chicago. Kelly had a problem. He was not a member of the Chicago City Council from which the next mayor was required to come from by law. So an ingenious political solution was proposed. Alderman Frank Corr would be elected by his colleagues. The State Legislature would then change the law regarding who was eligible for the office. With Corr's cooperation, he would then resign, Kelly would be elected, and Frank Corr could return as Alderman of the 17th Ward and once again, the legislature could reverse the law back again. This is exactly what happened, and for one month while events unfolded, Frank Corr was Mayor of the City of Chicago. He demonstrated a remarkable loyalty to the Council, to the Democratic Party and to the City of Chicago.

Edward Joseph Kelly (46th Mayor, 1933-1947)
Big city mayors do not come any more powerful, resourceful, or resilient than Ed Kelly, a longtime Democratic Party activist and leader. With his protégé, Pat Nash, he invigorated Chicago's political machine. The Bridgeport-born Kelly was President of the South Park Board when members of the Chicago City Council tapped him to succeed Mayor Anton Cermak following his assassination. Barred from the position as a non-member of the City Council, Pat Nash and the leaders of the State Legislature changed the law so that Kelly might be elected to the post. After his election, Kelly stepped in as Mayor and immediately the State Legislature changed the law back to what it had been. He spent the next fourteen years leading Chicago and acquiring a national

Mayor Anton Joseph Cermak
Mayor Frank J. Corr
Mayor Edward Joseph Kelly

First President of the Irish Free State William T. Cosgrave and Mayor William Hale Thompson, fur coated against the Chicago winter. January 22, 1928. DN-0084734, *Chicago Daily News* negatives collection, Chicago History Museum.

Mayor Ed Kelly and his political partner Pat Nash (on the left) broadcast on radio. Far to the right Alderman Jacob Arvey. Chicago History Museum, i20008.

Mayor Richard J. Daley addresses a crowd in the lobby of City Hall. Chicago History Museum, i31412.

Victory celebration for 14th Alderman Joseph P. Burke, congratulated by former 14th Ward Alderman— Judge James J. McDermott, Election Night, 1953.

reputation for political intelligence. When President Franklin Delano Roosevelt finished his second term in office and eschewed talk of a third term, it was Ed Kelly and his big-city mayor colleagues who stampeded the 1940 Democratic National Convention for FDR. Reluctantly, the president ran for a third term and led the nation when America was attacked at Pearl Harbor. At the Democratic National Convention in 1944, held once more in Chicago, Kelly and big-city bosses dumped Vice President Henry Wallace from the ticket for Roosevelt's fourth run for office. With Roosevelt's help, they dragooned Missouri Senator Henry S. Truman to be Vice President. Within months of the election, Roosevelt was dead, Truman was president and brought World War II to a strategic conclusion. During Kelly's first term in office he presided over the 1933 Century of Progress, the World's Fair celebrating Chicago's 100th anniversary of its birth.

Martin H. Kennelly (47th Mayor, 1947-1955)

As the clock was running out on Mayor Ed Kelly's political career, Democratic political leaders sought a quiet and squeaky clean businessman to change with the times. In the political world of post-World War II, Martin H. Kennelly was tailor-made for the job. The Bridgeport-born Kennelly was a prosperous Lake Shore Drive entrepreneur when he tossed his hat into the ring. He offered a different style of politics to Chicago. He was gentlemanly, courtly, refined and had none of the "smoke-filled back room" ways about him. Many looked on him as a reformer. Over the course of his two terms as mayor, political operatives had seen the wheels of urban government come to a grinding halt. Party leaders looked for an exit strategy for Kennelly as the election of 1955 approached. When their chief candidate, the powerful Finance Committee Chairman, and 14th Ward Alderman, Clarence Wagner was killed in an automobile accident, all eyes turned to the Chairman of the Cook County Democratic Central Committee—Richard J. Daley. He would reinvent Chicago's political machine.

Richard J. Daley (48th Mayor, 1955-1976)

Chicago's third Bridgeport-born mayor, Richard J. Daley, was something of an anomaly—growing up an only child in a southside Irish family. All his life Daley was a hard worker, a heavy lifter and a political loyalist. Mentored by Bridgeport Alderman "Big Joe" McDonough, Daley learned the nuances and realities of political survival in Chicago. He was nobody's fool. When McDonough was elected Cook County Treasurer in 1930, his right hand man, Richard J. Daley, was at his side, often running the show at the office. Daley's political career began in the Illinois General Assembly, ironically as a Republican in 1936. By 1938, he was a Democrat once again tried and true. In 1946 he suffered his only political defeat when he ran for Cook County Sheriff. But by the late 1940's, Daley was Committeeman of the historic 11th Ward. A graduate of DePaul University School of Law, Daley served as Clerk of Cook County in 1950 and Chairman of the Cook County Democratic Central Committee before his election as mayor in 1955. He would remain in office for the next 21 years, providing Chicago with dynamic and often aggressive leadership. He refused to permit Chicago to unravel as did other big rustbelt cities in the late 1950's and 1960's. He carried Chicago into the Jet Age and was instrumental in helping John Fitzgerald Kennedy become the President of the United States. Many political commentators see Daley as the last "Old Boss" urban politician. However, Chicagoans know this as a shallow judgment that can only be understood in its entirety in the present, more than 30 years after his death. Chicago is a vital, exciting, stable and manageable metropolis because in the past he set in place its foundation for urban survival. He always understood Chicago's urban character, seeing it as "a city of neighborhoods." His sudden death in 1976 reordered Chicago politics.

Michael A. Bilandic (49th Mayor, 1976-1979)

In the aftermath of Richard J. Daley's death, local politicians and Democratic Party strategists discovered there was no real successor to Daley's legacy. Instead the Chicago City Council sought out

Mayor Martin H. Kennelly
Mayor Richard Joseph Daley
Mayor Michael Anthony Bilandic

Mayor William Dever's
Funeral from St. Ita Church on
September 6, 1929
N. Broadway, DN-0089284.

Then State Senator,
Richard M. Daley and
his mother Eleanor
Guilfoyle Daley, with
John Cardinal Cody
at the funeral of
Mayor Richard J. Daley,
December 22, 1976

The longlines of the vigil all through the night, mourning Mayor Harold Washington, November 27-29, 1987.

a gentleman-caretaker, someone with whom they could cooperate and move ahead. Council President Pro Tem Wilson Frost asserted his right to assume the office of mayor on weak legal grounds. The Council did not concur and instead elected the alderman from Daley's own 11th Ward, Michael A. Bilandic. He was a soft spoken, highly intelligent, party loyalist and lawyer whom they could trust in the Office of Mayor. Bilandic would later run for a full term and was handily elected. However, his popularity ended abruptly when he took the blame for ineffective city snow removal following a great blizzard which paralyzed Chicago in 1979. Bilandic, however, would go on to have a distinguished career in both the Illinois Appellate and Supreme Courts. In recognition of his judicial achievements, the LaSalle Street home of the Illinois Supreme and Appellate Courts is named in his honor—the Michael A. Bilandic Building.

Jane Burke Byrne
(50th Mayor, 1979-1983)
Jane Byrne was a tough, savvy, urban independent with a superb track record working in John F. Kennedy's presidential campaign long before she was elected to public office. Throughout most of her career, she was a Democratic Party loyalist. Mentored by Richard J. Daley, himself, she, like him, had a talent for discerning the infighting always present in Chicago politics. She was fearless, aggressive and extremely bright. She served as Commissioner of Consumer Affairs for the City of Chicago during the administration of both Mayor Daley and Mayor Michael Bilandic. When she was summarily dismissed from this post by Bilandic, to her surprise, she did what she did best—she challenged the political establishment. When Bilandic's political career was buried by a Chicago snowfall, she picked herself up and challenged him at the polls, becoming Chicago's first female mayor. In a brilliant political move, to highlight conditions in Chicago's public housing, she and her husband, journalist Jay McMullen, moved into the Cabrini Green housing project thus attracting national media attention. When firefighters

threatened her with a walk-out, she stood up to them and ultimately paid the price in a first ever firefighter strike. Her political troubles increased when Richard M. Daley, the Cook County States Attorney, decided to challenge her in the 1983 mayoral election. So too did Southside Congressman Harold Washington. The real enmity was between Byrne and Daley. They set the political stage which saw Harold Washington become Chicago's first African American Mayor. Jane Byrne was a woman of her times and a product of her Chicago political roots. She may have been unable to understand the political realities of Chicago and succumbed to her failure to compromise.

Harold Washington
(51st Mayor, 1983-1987)
Harold Washington had a way with words—he could charm the birds from the trees. He captured the attention and the hearts of Chicagoans, black and white, rich and poor who were ready for a change. His historic 1983 election was a curious barometer of Chicago's political climate and the political infighting that paralyzed the City. Washington gave countless Chicagoans hope, and though his collision with members of the Chicago City Council gave birth to a new form of political maneuvering and gamesmanship. He was equal to the challenges. "Politics ain't Bean Bag," he was fond of saying. Even in the midst of the most virulent political debate, Washington never lacked a sense of humor. Confronting the majority vote of the "Vrdolyak 29," as his opposition in the City Council was known; he characterized their leadership not as racists (he knew better) but as bullies. His election to a second term granted him unmatched political control and hope in the future. On November 25, 1987 he collapsed and died from a massive heart attack in his fifth floor office. He was deeply mourned. For two days, more than 100,000 people filed past his casket in the lobby of City Hall. His jocularity and political acumen stand as his legacy to the people of the City he served and loved.

Mayor Harold Washington
Mayor David Duvall Orr

David Orr (52nd Mayor, 1987)

David Orr is currently the Clerk of Cook County, but in 1987 he was Alderman of the 49th Ward when he was catapulted into history as Mayor of the City of Chicago following the death of Harold Washington. A longtime political activist and campaigner with a deep independent streak, David Orr was mayor for one week, from November 25 to December 2, 1987. He chaired only one City Council meeting, December 1, 1987, which to this day stands as one of the most dramatic, aggressive and volatile political encounters in Chicago history. It lasted until 4:00 a.m. on December 2nd. When the meeting adjourned, the Chicago City Council had elected its second African American mayor.

Eugene Sawyer (53rd Mayor, 1987-1989)

Chicago may never have had a more reluctant mayor than Eugene Sawyer. A member of the Chicago City Council from the 6th Ward, he was a quiet, taciturn regular organization loyalist. He was also the answer to a dilemma. Following the death of Chicago's first African American Mayor, Harold Washington, it was important to continue the political and cultural continuity that Washington had created. But the majority aldermen needed a leader they could work with, which excluded many of the potential candidates. While the streets around City Hall were crowded with concerned citizens that historic night, it took much encouragement to convince Eugene Sawyer to accept the nomination. He would serve out the remaining two years of Washington's term.

Richard M. Daley (54th Mayor, 1989-Present)

The fifth Chicago mayor to rise from the southside Irish enclave of Bridgeport, Richard M. Daley, had been Cook County's aggressive, tough, intelligent States Attorney since 1980. Following the political upheavals of the previous Washington years and its aftermath, Daley's brand of urban stability was attractive. His success in the Illinois State Legislature and as Chief Prosecutor of Cook County laid the groundwork for his successful 1989 election to the office his father held for 21 years. Since then, Daley has equaled his father's longevity in office. Like him, he has reinvented the urban cityscape of Chicago. While his political patina is larger and more rainbow-tinged, Daley the younger is a man of his times and understands the municipal character of Chicago. He has enhanced Chicago's reputation as an international city, a favorite tourist destination known for its stunning architecture, fine art and dazzling lakefront splendor. Since he took office more than two decades ago, he has become Chicago's "greenest" mayor, planting more than 500,000 trees across the face of urban Chicago and even creating a green roof for Chicago's historic City Hall.

Mayor Eugene Sawyer
Mayor Richard M. Daley

Mayor Richard J. Daley
waves his green fedora in the
Chicago St. Patrick's Day
parade which he reinvented
down State Street.

White Sox Manager
Ozzie Guillen and
Mayor Richard M. Daley
celebrate the 2005
Sox World Series victory

Holabird & Roche and the Chicago School of Architecture

"In architecture as in all other operative arts, the end must direct the operation. The end is to build well. Well building has three conditions: Commodity, Firmness and Delight."
Henry Watton

The architectural team of Holabird & Roche fashioned the neo-classical design and soaring contours of Chicago's seventh City Hall. They set in motion a potent and powerful architectural form for Chicago's most important municipal building. Their combined genius wrapped the function and endeavors of urban government within the skin of ancient Greece. They placed a highly-crafted historical stone edifice squarely on the streetscape of Chicago.

Its purpose was set. Its function was derivative. But its environment was radically different from what anyone had even seen on the floor of the Prairie. Their intention was very clear—to place around the everyday functions of Chicago's municipal government the highest form of ancient design with modern updates. It was meant to recall the enduring and regal days of Greece's most exciting and elegant heyday; a time when democracy—a gift from the Greeks—first reared its most noble head. Who were these remarkable Chicago architects? What led them to this grandiose concept within which government was surrounded by man's most noble architectural ideals? What influences shaped their architectural vision? And how critical was their professional relationship with the vision of William LeBaron Jenney, their former employer—the man who invented the urban skyscraper?

William Holabird and Martin Roche were contemporaries and part of a generation of American architects deeply influenced by the legacy that flowed from the great pioneers of American design. Their legacy to Chicago is no less than the school of architectural design known around the world as "The Chicago School." Holabird was born in Almira, New York in 1854 and raised in St. Paul, Minnesota in a military family. His father, Samuel Beckley Holabird, was an officer in the United States Army and rose to the rank of Brigadier General. Holabird, himself, enrolled at West Point in 1873, but found the discipline and curriculum not to his liking. He resigned in 1875. He married and moved to Chicago that same year and began employment with William LeBaron Jenney. It was here during his architectural apprenticeship that he first met Martin Roche, as well as Ossian Simonds, both of whom would become later professional partners.

The Cleveland-born Martin Roche moved to Chicago as a child of two in 1857 and was a fine cabinetmaker by the time he was a teen. He was educated at the Armour Institute (now the Illinois Institute of Technology). At only 17 years of age he was employed by William LeBaron Jenney in 1872 and went on to become head draftsman at his Chicago firm, as well as a skilled designer of decorative plans. By 1881 Roche had joined the firm set up by Holabird and Simonds. After two strenuous years which included Roche designing furniture to keep the practice funded, Simonds made the decision to go on his own. The firm then became known as Holabird & Roche, a partnership that would play a central role in the designing of a modern downtown Chicago. It was instrumental in the development of many of Chicago's most refined skyscrapers that make the urban skyline so robust, quintessentially American and singularly Chicagoan.

The influence of William LeBaron Jenney (1832-1907) and his steel-framed skyscraper cannot be underestimated on both Holabird & Roche and the aesthetic of their future architectural vision. A colleague of Jenney's once described the motivation of the architecture like this— *While he felt he was contributing to the making of new architectural forms, that was not his motive...His main purpose was to create structural features which increased the effective floor areas and made it possible to secure more daylight with the building.*

It was always said that Jenney sought efficiency and economy in his buildings; most tended to be simple expressions of the underlying metal skeleton within.

It is fair to say that in Chicago's seventh City Hall Holabird & Roche were faithful to their mentor's esthetic value, though they embellished the Grecian temple's exterior with a dazzling sense of grandeur. Yet their interior functionality and efficiency would have delighted Jenney, Chicago's ground breaking architect.

Holabird died in 1923 and Roche in 1927. Holabird's son, John A. Holabird (1886-1945) and John Wellborn Root, Jr., (1887-1963), himself the son of a well-known Chicago architect, reorganized the firm in 1929. Since then Holabird & Root has continued to make fresh contributions to the cityscape of Chicago, none more demonstrative of Chicago's character than the Chicago Board of Trade and the Palmolive Building.

Other Works Designed by Holabird & Roche | Holabird & Root

Graceland Cemetery Chapel, 1888
4001 N. Clark Street

Tacoma Building, 1889

Fort Sheridan, 1890

Monadnock Building (southern part), 1893
53 W. Jackson Boulevard

Marquette Building, 1895
140 S. Dearborn Street

Gage Group Buildings, 1899
24 S. Michigan Avenue

University Club of Chicago, 1908
76 E. Monroe Street

University of Illinois Ice Arena, 1913
406 E. Armory Avenue, Champaign IL

Three Arts Clubs, 1914
47 W. Division Street

Memorial Stadium (Champaign), 1923
1402 S. 1st Street Champaign, IL

Soldier Field, 1924
425 E. McFetridge Drive

Pedestals for Ivan Mestrovic's
The Bowman and Spearman
statues, 1926

Palmer House Hotel, 1927
17 E. Monroe Street

Stevens Hotel, 1927
720 S. Michigan Avenue

Daily News Building, 1928
2 N. Riverside Plaza

333 N. Michigan Avenue,
1928

Palmolive Building, 1929
919 N. Michigan Avenue

Century of Progress Exposition,
1929-1933

Chicago Board of Trade, 1930
141 W. Jackson Boulevard

American sculptor John Flanagan's Bas-reliefs of The Four Great Features of Municipal Government: The Playground, The Parks, Water Supply System and Public Schools.

Design for expanded
City Hall addition of a
multi-storied Criminal Courts
building soaring above.
It never came to be. Mayor
Anton Cermak relocated the
project to his constituency
at 26th Street and
California Avenue.
Drawing by Holabird & Roche
master-draftman Gilbert Hall.

Chicago Alderman aboard the *Wendella*
in the Chicago River, 1943

Edward M. Burke is a former Chicago Police Officer; the Dean of the Chicago City Council; Alderman of Chicago's 14th Ward for the past 40-years; the Chairman of the Chicago City Council's Committee on Finance; the Democratic Ward Committeeman of the 14th Ward; the Chairman of the Judicial Slate Making Committee of the Democratic Party of Cook County; Chairman, Board of Trustees, Policemen's and Firemen's Death Benefit Fund; a practicing attorney, partner in the Chicago law firm of Klafter and Burke; a member of the Council of Regents of Loyola University Chicago; a member of the Sovereign Military Order of Malta; a Knight Commander of the Equestrian Order of the Holy Sepulchre of Jerusalem; a student of Chicago history; a noted public speaker and Co-Author of *Inside the Wigwam— Chicago Presidential Conventions, 1860-1996; and End of Watch-Chicago Police Killed in the Line of Duty 1853-2006*. At present he is completing work on *Return to Quarters— Chicago Firefighters Killed in the Line of Duty 1857-2009*, scheduled for publication in spring 2010. He was also a contributor to *Chicago: City of the Century*, The American Experience, WGBH Boston. He is married to Illinois Supreme Court Justice Anne M. Burke.

Thomas J. O'Gorman is a painter, architectural artist and a Chicago writer, as well as Assistant to the Chairman of the Chicago City Council Committee on Finance, and its Director of Policy and Communications. He is also Historian-in-Residence of the Irish Fellowship Club of Chicago. Formerly a Managing Editor at the *World of Hibernia Magazine*, and a former contributor to *Town and Country Magazine*; he is the author of *Park Life, the Summer of 1977 at Comiskey Park* (2000); *One Hundred Years —The History of the Irish Fellowship Club of Chicago* (2001); *New Spaces from Salvage* (2002); *The Houses We live In* (2003) and *Architecture in Detail: Chicago* (2004); *Frank Lloyd Wright's Chicago* (2004); *Chicago in Photographs* (2005) and *Strange but True: Chicago* (2005). He is co-author of *End of Watch, Chicago Police Killed in the Line-of-Duty, 1853-2006*, published in (2007). Scheduled for an early 2010 release are *Then and Now Chicago– From the Air; and Dublin–Then and Now*, both by Anova Books, London. At present he is completing work on *Return to Quarters–Chicago Firefighters Killed in the Line of Duty 1857-2009*, scheduled for publication in spring 2010. A contributor to *Chicago: City of the Century*, The American Experience, WGBH Boston, he writes and lectures on Chicago history and architecture; 18th Century Irish architecture; and 20th Century Irish painting. A Dublin exhibition of his paintings in early 2010 is planned.

at the right
Thomas J. O'Gorman
detail of *Chicago's City Hall at 100*, 2009
Acrylic on linen, 60 x 40 inches